T0197307

BREAK THROUGH

BREAK THROUGH

What Cabin Crew Can Teach You
About **Leadership, Teamwork** and
Customer Contact

Thomas Gelmi

BREAKTHROUGH
WHAT CABIN CREW CAN TEACH YOU ABOUT LEADERSHIP, TEAMWORK AND CUSTOMER CONTACT

iUniverse books may be ordered through booksellers or by contacting:

iUniverse
1663 Liberty Drive
Bloomington, IN 47403
www.iuniverse.com
1-800-Authors (1-800-288-4677)

Because of the dynamic nature of the Internet, any web addresses or links contained in this book may have changed since publication and may no longer be valid. The views expressed in this work are solely those of the author and do not necessarily reflect the views of the publisher, and the publisher hereby disclaims any responsibility for them.

Any people depicted in stock imagery provided by Getty Images are models, and such images are being used for illustrative purposes only.
Certain stock imagery © Getty Images.

ISBN: 978-1-5320-7127-0 (sc)
ISBN: 978-1-5320-7128-7 (e)

Print information available on the last page.

iUniverse rev. date: 03/27/2019

CONTENTS

//

Introduction ix
Check-In 1
Pre-Flight (Part 1) 6
Personal Competence 9
    Self-Exploration 10
    Self-Awareness 22
    Self-Management 33
Interpersonal Competence 54
    Situational and Social Awareness 55
    Communication 64
    Relationship Management 78
Pre-Flight (Part 2) 96
Destination Leadership 99
    Above The Clouds 99
    Challenges In Leadership 102
    Breakthrough In Leadership 107
Destination Teamwork 125
    Above The Clouds 125
Destination Customer Contact 140
    Above The Clouds 140
    Challenges In Customer Contact 143
    Breakthrough In Customer Contact 146
Destination Private Life 154
    Above The Clouds 154
    Challenges In Private Life 156
    Breakthrough In Private Life 159
Safe Landing 167
end notes 177
Acknowledgments 181
Index 183
Bibliography 187
Thomas Gelmi 191

For Lisa & Dario

INTRODUCTION
//

When attempting to find the right title for the English version of this book, I was faced with a linguistic challenge. The original German version's title is "Durchstarten" which has a double meaning: "Durchstarten" is an aviation term and translates to "Go-Around", which describes a flight procedure in which a final approach is aborted and does not end with the landing of the aircraft. Instead, the pilot moves the power levers forward, retracts the landing gear and flaps and goes into climb in order to make a second, safe final approach. The most common reasons for a go-around maneuver are: No visual contact at the so-called minimum - the altitude at which the pilots have to be able to see the runway or the approach lights, heavy gusts shortly before touchdown, or an aircraft which has not cleared the runway on time.

In everyday language, the term is associated with getting started, giving your best, gaining momentum, or: a breakthrough as in being successful. Since the direct translation "Go-Around" doesn't have the colloquial meaning, we chose "Breakthrough" for the English book, which has a perfect association with aviation as well:

"Just before you break through the sound barrier, the cockpit shakes the most."
CHUCK YEAGER

In October 1947, Chuck Yeager[1] was the first person to break through the sound barrier in his Bell X-1. When asked about this experience, he described how just before breaking through the sound barrier, the cockpit shook the most. Apparently, things immediately calmed down after that moment. When I imagine the massive increase of resistance and pressure imposed on the structures before the breakthrough, some parallels with work and life in general come to mind. Have you ever experienced how in particularly difficult situations, an almost sudden sensation of breakthrough can be felt after a certain (low-)point has been reached? This is indeed what I am referring to in this book when I talk about a breakthrough in leadership, teamwork, and customer contact.

With all this in mind, I would like to invite, encourage and hopefully inspire you to break through your personal sound barrier, through what keeps you from being even more successful. May you be enabled to be more effective in your interactions, faced with less friction and resistance and to reach your goals more smoothly, with less "shaking of the cockpit".

This book does not claim to be scientifically substantiated. There are enough other authors who have covered that field. Nor is it based on extensive studies, academic analyses or assessments. There are plenty of those as well and I will refer to some of them. This book is mainly based on my personal experience in collaborating with people and in dealing with myself. I do not claim to have found the be-all and end-all answer – not at all. Like all of us, I am on a journey, a journey which eventually will lead to myself. Or in other words, the beautiful part of aging is that the older you become, the more you start resembling yourself.

Nor do I re-invent the wheel in this book or inspire you with ground-breaking innovations. As a matter of fact, most of what you will read here could be considered common sense. This leads me to my main motivation for writing this book. Throughout all the years in which I have dealt with people in the most diverse roles and functions, I have missed exactly that over and over again: benevolence and common sense. Not that the intention was not there – but too often, our ego gets in the way and puts us in the fog of unconsciousness, which often complicates matters.

In my opinion, many of the issues we currently face in companies can be traced back to a lack of real, authentic and human connection. There is a lack of empathy, integration, understanding and solution focus. Instead, we often experience cold, dividing and egocentric behavior, uncontrolled outbursts of anger, sarcasm, and irony. And last, but not least, often the source of all misery: the argument over who is right. So, often, there is a winner, but on the other hand, there are many losers. I believe that our world, and I specifically mean the business world, is in a state of imbalance in several ways.

The way to better balance initially leads to ourselves. Once we fix our relationship to our inner self, many other issues resolve themselves. This requires the willingness to at least consider it an option that others are not to blame for certain situations. That we can't just wait for circumstances to change, for others to finally change their behavior, maybe even recognize their faults. And it takes the courage to take a closer look at yourself, set out for starting to truly get to know yourself. With everything that entails. "There is nothing in nature that does not grow from the inside out", a Native Indian saying states. Likewise, the journey to greater success in professional and personal relationships first takes us towards the inside and starts with ourselves.

I often tell the participants of my seminars: "You are participants. Therefore, take the parts that are helpful for you and simply leave all other parts behind." I would like for you to approach this book the same way. Take and utilize the parts that are valuable, helpful and meaningful to you.

Let me share a short story: *A professor went on a long hike into the mountains to go see a famous Zen monk. When the professor found him, he politely introduced himself, named all his academic titles and asked the monk for a special lesson. "Would you like some tea", the monk asked him. "Sure, thank you", the professor replied. The old monk poured him some tea. The cup was full, but the monk continued pouring until the cup overflowed and the tea dropped from the table onto the floor. "Enough", the professor proclaimed. "Can't you see that the cup is already full? It can't hold any more." The professor answered: "Just like this cup, you are filled up with your knowledge and your prejudices. In order to learn something new, you first have to empty your cup."*

Consequently, I invite you to empty your cup and come along with me on a journey with an open mind. I will gladly accompany you for part of your journey and serve as your personal flight attendant. Get on board and take a seat. For take-off, please fasten your seatbelt and ensure that the backrest of your seat is in an upright position and the table in front of you is folded away. I am excited to have you on board and wish you an exciting and enlightening journey.

CHECK-IN
//

Prior to finding my professional calling, I tried out a few other things, which is why my biography contains some rather colorful milestones. In combination with the last 15 years, one of them is of particular importance in forming the golden thread for this book: The time I spent with Swissair, the former Swiss airline. I was there for seven years, from 1994 until 2001, when the entire fleet was grounded and the remaining parts of Swissair and the airline Crossair were merged into the foundation of Swiss International Airlines, which is now part of the Lufthansa Group.

For Swissair, I served as Maître de Cabine, a position other airlines call Purser, or Inflight Manager. As the M/C – the commonly used acronym – together with my crew, I was responsible for passenger safety and excellent service in all compartments on board. I worked and travelled on all international routes, between Los Angeles and Tokyo and Oslo and Cape Town. I managed crews of high diversity regarding age, cultural and professional background. We were a truly colorful group and even though there were eventually 3,500 of us flight attendants, we felt like we were all part of one big family.

The diversity I experienced among our passengers was even greater. They literally came from all over the world. During that time, I met many fascinating people and learned a lot about human beings. I still benefit from those encounters and experiences, particularly when it comes to my professional activities.

I assume that you have sat on an airplane before and are familiar with the situation: You and, depending on the type of aircraft, just a few or up to 800 other people share a very tight space at an altitude of around 10,000 meters or 35,000 feet. This poses a quite unnatural situation which most people perceive as stressful in one way or another. Considering the tight space conditions, the fact that there would be no chance of survival outside the aircraft and the experience of occasional turbulences, the situation can be perceived as intimidating or even threatening. Additionally, many people feel a loss of control and therefore as though they are at the mercy of the crew. This means there is a certain tension which manifests itself differently in each person: one may talk a lot, the other drinks more and others go quiet or become very demanding.

This tube, packed with people, actually resembles a small company, with everything that entails. There is direct customer contact, there are teams who cooperate in different functions and across various departments and there is leadership happening on different levels. The cabin crew fulfills a dual role in this system. On the one hand, they ensure the passengers' safety on board and on the other hand, they take care of the passengers in the sense of providing them with services. Even though most passengers perceive the service role as the most prevalent one, passenger safety has the highest priority. What's more: Safety is the actual reason why there are flight attendants on board in the first place. Aviation authorities require a minimum crew on board depending on the number of doors and emergency exits as well as the number of passengers on board. For example, it must be ensured that a fully booked aircraft can be evacuated within 90 seconds using only half of the available emergency exits.

So, this often underestimated profession presents major challenges for the self- and relationship-competence of the crew members. The term "unruly passenger" is one that could unfortunately increasingly be heard during the last years I worked for Swissair. A passenger was considered "unruly" when he or she repeatedly ignored instructions given by the crew, insulted the personnel or refused to follow regulations. About half of those cases were caused by the consumption of alcohol or tobacco – despite the smoking ban on board. We even experienced situations of vulgar remarks and attacks on the cabin crew. The international airline passengers association (IAPA for short) already spoke of 50,000 annual incidents worldwide in 2001, when I left Swissair. In that year alone, Swissair had recorded 572 incidents involving unruly passengers on board their aircraft. This meant the number had doubled compared to 1996, the year in which the statistical recording of inappropriate behavior of airline passengers started.

This special environment required the early detection of problems, whether they were of a technical or human interaction related nature. Issues had to be anticipated and de-escalated in a timely way. In a figurative sense, we had to provide a maximum of pro-active fire prevention measures in order to avoid having to extinguish a fire in a reactive sense. Whenever there was an actual problem, it had to be resolved – quickly. Without being able to obtain help from the outside. And while preserving the underlying relationship, because any form of escalation could have easily gotten out of control.

More Human Kindness

Nowadays, I concern myself with the challenges executives and employees in other companies have to overcome. For many of those enterprises, the situation has become more VUCA (volatile, uncertain, complex and ambiguous) over the course of the last few years. Moreover, a big share of the working hours of executives and employees is taken up by resolving conflicts and managing their consequences.

Uncooperative behavior and escalated conflicts pose an enormous financial burden for businesses year after year and potential economic profits are destroyed by such frictional losses.

More kindness in leadership and cooperation is what I – and many others - believe to be needed. I am not talking about some kind of wellness trip nor yet another way of extracting higher output from the employees, the human resources. Rather, I am referring to the humane attitude which is shaped by appreciation and mutual respect. Kindness which is displayed in small and big acts of daily collaboration. It is an attitude which is deeply rooted in each and single manager and employee alike and thus entails high self-competence as a solid foundation.

A culture shaped in this manner is the prerequisite for an emotional bond between employees and their company, which in turn is directly linked to the emotional bond with the most important people employees interact with: Customers. In times of a continuously increasing comparability of products and services, it is the employees who make the difference in customer experience and can become a crucial competitive advantage – or disadvantage if they do not display the necessary attitude. Only content and engaged employees who identify with their company and its services are able to shift their focus to the outside world, the customers, and allow them to experience real, authentic customer orientation. In this process, the quality and level of leadership is an essential component.

What if employees and managers were able to significantly reduce the number of conflicts through higher personal and interpersonal competence as well as more attentive communication and cooperation? What if employees were able to de-escalate acute conflicts in the workplace? What kind of impact would that have on a company's productivity and profitability?

Well, I have got good news for you – especially if you believe that this is about "soft skills". This is not a matter of "nice to have". In the end, this is about increasing economic success – which, in the end, entails hard facts.

We Are All Service Providers

I am convinced that having a service oriented mindset as a basic attitude brings many advantages, opens doors and serves as a key success factor, particularly when it comes to leadership and collaboration. Being a service provider does not necessarily mean that this has to be of submissive character, as it may seem to some people. "We are Ladies and Gentlemen, serving Ladies and Gentlemen" is the central motto of the renowned Ritz-Carlton Hotel Company and exemplifies a service culture on an equal footing, the kind I am referring to.

When you fulfill a task for your superior, you are his or her service provider. When you give your best in taking care of a task for your colleagues, you are their service provider. There even is the common term of "servant leadership" which describes the service attitude taken from a superior's perspective; not just towards the next hierarchical level or the customer – where the service orientation is obvious - but also towards employees. That kind of mindset seeks to create an optimum environment allowing the team as a whole and each individual employee to excel. Viewed from that angle, leadership can be seen in a new light.

Daniel Goleman's[2] research shows that business results in companies increase by one percent when the service factor – the factor which measures how friendly and helpful a company's employees act – increases by two percent. Independent of whether the company operated in the service industry or not.

Another model which shows the correlation between committed employees and profitability is the *Harvard Value Profit Chain*[3]. Based on the assumption that ultimately, we are all service providers, even when we are not working for a service provider, this correlation is relevant in a direct or indirect way – and this includes employees who do not have direct customer contact.

The Journey Starts With Ourselves

One could simply say: "Alright, then lets simply take another communication course, another leadership course and practice these tools and techniques." That certainly is something that can be and actually is done. However, my experience has shown that those measures merely touch the surface. When someone has not reached a certain point in his personal development at which he applies the "tools and techniques" based on the necessary underlying attitude, then he will not be effective. In the worst case, which unfortunately happens all too often, a person will try something new for a few days only to fall back into old thought and behavioral patterns because "it's not working".

Instead, we need to develop genuine interpersonal competence, that is, the ability to enter into authentic contact with others, establish relationships and maintain them even under challenging circumstances. In order to accomplish that, we need to do more than learn tools and study techniques. The journey needs to start with ourselves. First, we must be authentic and turn within. In a second step, we can stand our ground and are able to turn towards the outside and establish genuine contact with others.

In order to develop our relationship (or interpersonal) competence, we need a solid foundation. This foundation is called "self-competence", also known as "personal competence". We need to strengthen each individual in his or her self-competence, in his interaction and contact with himself. Therefore, the underlying overall concept of this book is called *InterPersonal Competence*. The unusual spelling intends to stress the fact that *personal competence* is an essential component of *interpersonal competence*.

Image 1: InterPersonal Competence

PRE-FLIGHT (PART 1)

//

Luckily, I did not know what was awaiting me that day when I arrived, early, as usual, at the Operations Center at Zurich airport. The "OPS" is where the flight personnel meets, cockpit and cabin crews, to prepare their flights, obtain all necessary flight information and hold the flight briefing. It was a beautiful fall morning and my schedule for the day listed a short flight to Frankfurt and back to Zurich. Due to a large book fair in Frankfurt and the expected high volume of passengers, an Airbus A330 had been dispatched, which was an exception for such a short flight.

The service center provided me with all important flight information. This included the crew list with all names and ranks, transitory operations information – abbreviated "TOI" – with the passenger numbers, special passenger profiles (VIPs, frequent flyers, unattended minors, wheelchairs, special medical needs, special meals etc.) and other information pertaining to the flight. Contrary to my expectations, only around three fourths of the seats were booked.

A good mix of senior and young flight attendants met for the crew briefing which I led. I assigned functions and work positions for each crew member, communicated my focus and expectations for the flight and let the crew know what they could expect from me in return. The atmosphere was good and, as customary, shortly thereafter we met with the cockpit crew at the crew exit where we were picked up by a crew bus and taken to the aircraft.

The big twin-engine plane was shining in the morning sun when we climbed the flight of stairs and, once on board, everything went forward as usual. The cabin was prepared for boarding. I checked the onboard electronics, tested the various systems and continuously coordinated with the cockpit and ground staff. At the given time, I gave the OK for boarding and shortly thereafter, the first passengers came walking down the gangway to the aircraft. Boarding was completed without any special incidents. One of the flight attendants had counted the passengers and her numbers matched those of the passenger list and the ground staff, so we were good to go.

I checked once again with the cockpit crew and then closed the door. The captain used the intercom and gave the instruction "Cabin crew: door selectors to armed". This command prompts those flight attendants who are responsible for a door to move a yellow lever at the door so that the emergency escape slide/raft is armed.

From that moment on, if a door handle is turned, the door opens pneumatically and within a matter of seconds, the emergency escape slide inflates so that the plane can be evacuated. Immediately following the command and its execution, the flight attendants perform a cross-check to verify that the door across the aisle has been set on alarmed correctly.

The moment the door was closed was also the moment we felt that the large corporation of Swissair turned into our own little enterprise in which I, together with the two pilots and the cabin crew, was responsible for the safety of our passengers and the service quality on board. Particularly the former should become especially challenging on that flight.

We were already taxiing towards the runway while my colleagues in the various sections of the aircraft checked the cabin and secured the galleys for take-off. One after the other, I received the OK from the responsible flight attendants through the intercom and passed it on to the pilots: "Cabin and Galleys secured." We were ready for take-off. I sat down on the jump seat at my station and started my "one minute of silent review". This is a form of mental training used by flight attendants during the critical phases of take-off and landing. Each cabin crew member focuses and makes himself aware of the situation. The purpose of the technique is to make the flight attendant aware of his assigned work position, its implications and emergency equipment. It includes a mental review of potential scenarios and subsequent appropriate actions in order to ensure an immediate and correct reaction in case of an emergency.

"Take-off in one minute", the captain's voice could be heard announcing the imminent take-off. The aircraft entered the runway and lined up with the center line. The seatbelt signs were turned off and turned back on once. For the crew, that was the sign for take-off.

The pilots pushed the thrust levers forward and the heavy aircraft was put into motion. This meant highest concentration for us in the cabin. "Expect the unexpected" was an attitude which we had been prepared for in our basic training. This particularly applied to the take-off and landing phases. We were wide awake, focused and paid careful attention with all senses to any kind of irregularities. That morning, we took off on runway 16 heading south, took a wide left turn shortly after take-off and were soon high above the airport, on our way towards Frankfurt.

That was the moment it happened. We were still climbing and I had my seat belt fastened when the phone at my station rang. I picked it up and answered:

"Thomas, Station 12". "Claudia, Station 14", my colleague said at the other end of the line. "Thomas, you have to come back here immediately. Someone is going crazy!" I asked what exactly she meant, but she just replied: "Just get here. Hurry!"

I could feel my body catapulting to maximum performance readiness within seconds. My pulse leaped and I felt the adrenaline rushing through my veins. I unbuckled my seatbelt, stood up and told my colleague on the opposite side/across the aisle: "I have to go to the back, there is a problem!" Thanks to the curtains between the compartments being open for take-off, I was able to quickly see what my colleague was talking about. In the back of the cabin, a male passenger had stood up and was randomly beating on the backrests of other passengers' seats, insulting and threatening them in the worst way. The man was speaking English and he appeared to be from the Middle East. In the background, I could see the puzzled faces of my colleagues and all around me I saw the scared looks of the other passengers.

To be continued ...

PERSONAL COMPETENCE

//

Personal competence as referred to in this chapter essentially comprises three main aspects:

1. Self-Exploration

The rational perception of yourself. Do you know yourself – not in a philosophical sense, but rather in a practical way? Do you truly know your strengths? Can you name your core competencies? Do you really know what makes you unique, what distinguishes you and what you are better at than others? Are you aware of the fundamental values that determine your daily actions and decisions? Do you know your own convictions and beliefs?

2. Self-Awareness

Literally. Are you aware of yourself – at all times, in any given moment? Are you so much in touch with yourself that you can feel your emotional state? At what point do you recognize anger? In its early stages of development or when the pressure cooker explodes and an involved relationship is possibly damaged, or even destroyed? Are you in touch and in an amicable relationship with yourself?

3. Self-Management

If you know yourself well and continuously stay in touch with yourself, one question remains. Are you able to adequately handle your resources and emotions? Can you manage your energy in an optimal way and do you recognize the signs of stumbling into an excessively straining or even overwhelming situation? And, if you recognize your anger at an early stage, are you able to express it in a controlled and relationship-preserving manner to avoid an implosion or explosion, depending on your personality?

Image 2: Personal Competence

SELF-EXPLORATION
///

Gnothi Seauton – "Know thyself" – is an often quoted inscription in the forecourt of the Temple of Apollo at Delphi. It is attributed to Chilon of Sparta, one of the "Seven Sages". This means even the ancient Greeks knew of the importance of knowing who we are.

What lies behind the idea of self-exploration can be illustrated with the image of an iceberg. Only the tip of an iceberg, about 10% of its volume, is visible above the water. So, an impressive 90% are not recognizable at first glance, but only when you take a closer look, diving deeper into all that lies below the surface of the water. In shipping, failing to observe those hidden parts can lead to accidents, which is why sensitive devices are used for their detection.

Applied to human beings, this means you have to explore and take a closer look in order to understand. You can imagine: The tip of the iceberg is equivalent to the behavior you are aware of and which others can see. Below the "water surface" lie the unconscious parts of how you think and feel, your subconscious inner reactions as well as your values, personal beliefs and needs.

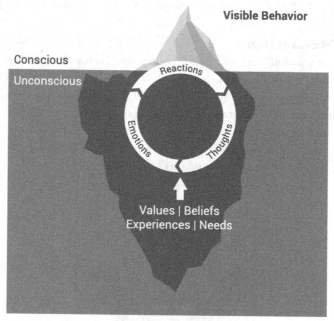

Image 3: The Iceberg of the Self

Even though we are often unaware of these aspects below the surface, they have a significant impact on the behavior we show at the tip of the iceberg. Hence, if you would like to gain greater understanding of yourself and the way you behave, then making yourself more aware of these unconscious parts is very helpful. This process can take different forms. The aspect of self-exploration focuses on a rather rational view of yourself which mainly requires knowing who you are. Here, we first address the knowledge of qualities that distinguish and make you unique which are identified through systematic exploration and reflection.

In my work as a coach and consultant I keep seeing that this level of knowledge among my clients is not very high. In many cases, people are not really sure who they are. When I ask them: "Who are you, what do you stand for? What distinguishes you from others?", they start quoting their resume. Obviously, the same thing happens in a job interview when a potential employer asks: "Who are you? Tell us about yourself." Then the answer is the resume: "I have worked here and there, done this and that, passed this apprenticeship and possess this degree, that certificate and these diplomas."

However, what matters to the potential employer? In the end, he wants to see the competencies the applicant is equipped with. Competence, as opposed to qualification, only becomes visible in the doing. I am sure you know people who are very good at what they are doing even though they may not have the "officially" required qualification. In many cases, they are autodidacts – people who have acquired competence through practical doing. On the other hand, there are people who are highly qualified, very knowledgeable, yet unable to translate that knowledge into competence. They may be good theorists and able to explain why and how something works and still not necessarily develop the corresponding practical competence.

We acquire up to 70 percent of what we are capable of - our competencies - on an informal path[4]. This means: by getting up in the morning, stepping out into the world, facing and meeting challenges. With our family, in our spare time, sports or in social commitment or volunteer work. We continuously develop new competencies. This turns our biography into a treasure chest. If you are able to clearly express your core competencies and qualities – because you know them – then you are also able to effectively position yourself in an internal or external application process and refreshingly distinguish yourself from the other applicants.

Moreover, this solid knowledge enables you to strengthen your personal identity, align your potential with changes in the job market and actively shape the transfer of individual competencies between personal life, education and professional activities. Thus, you are able to design your career path yourself in a targeted and active manner instead of passively having career decisions made for you. All of this can take place based on the assumption and realization that continuous change increasingly becomes a natural part of our professional life and you are not helplessly exposed to these changes.

Prerequisites For Self-Exploration

First of all, you obviously need to be aware of the necessity of knowing yourself. Then, it takes the conscious decision of wanting to get to know yourself better. Furthermore, it takes curiosity and courage to seriously take a closer look and deal with yourself – strong and weak points alike. And you need to be willing to accept outside perspectives and external perceptions as being just as real as your own.

As a matter of fact, a self-image can exist without the willingness to deal with yourself and compare your own perceptions with those of others. However, this self-image can easily be distorted. If you would like to see some impressive examples of distorted self-images, then watch shows such as "America's Got Talent" where you can see people who seem to have a self-image which is rather different from how the rest of the world sees them - to put it mildly.

What Is Your Reason To Get Up In The Morning?

Have you ever thought about the purpose of your life? I admit, that is a big question which each of us has to find their own answer to. However, to me, the answer is clear: I find my sense of purpose in life in discovering what constitutes me at the core of my existence as a human being – my essence; in expressing this essence as best as possible and thereby contributing to a greater good. This concept is displayed in the Japanese principle of "Ikigai". Put simply, it describes the feeling of having something, a sense of purpose which is worth getting up for. The often lengthy and thorough process of self-exploration in the search of *Ikigai* is deeply rooted in the Japanese culture. It is a very personal affair and its result can differ greatly from one individual to another. Once someone has found his *Ikigai*, he is rewarded with a sense of joy and inner contentment.

The Ikigai principle is graphically displayed with four circles which overlap in the center. On the left is the circle of qualities: What are you really good at? Maybe better than many others? At the top, you find the circle of preferences: What do you like, what do you enjoy doing, what do you love? What you are good at and what you love merges in the overlap and constitutes your passion. We move on to the third circle: what the world needs. The overlap of what you love and what the world needs creates your mission. The fourth circle displays what the world is willing to pay you for. The combination of what the world needs and what you can be paid for forms your vocation. In the center, where all circles overlap, you find your *Ikigai*. Your purpose in life.

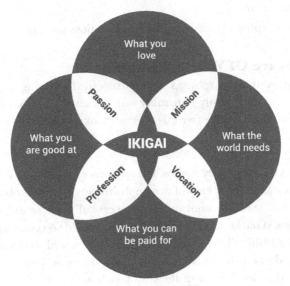

Image 4: "IKIGAI"

In a process of self-discovery or self-exploration, it is helpful to start by gradually and systematically exploring the first two areas. In doing so, a structured process which I will describe below has proven to be a successful tool.

1. *Taking a look at your own history. Where do you come from?*
2. *Taking a look at the present: Who have you become through your history?*
3. *Taking a look ahead: Where do you want to go?*

Where Do You Come From?

The first step, a systematic look back, is an unfamiliar one for many people. Of course, you know your own biography. However, other than in the course of drafting a resume or curriculum vitae, have you ever actually and systematically reflected upon your past? Have you ever thought about the various areas in life and asked yourself: What have I gone through thus far? What were the most important milestones and decisions that set a new course in my life so far? What kind of events have left a deep and lasting mark? The best approach to dealing with these questions is to draw a time line of your life on which you write down everything that comes to your mind regarding the following areas of life.

// Professional environment: Your professional development, your career path,education and training;

// Personal environment: Personal relationships, family, friends, acquaintances etc.;

// Leisure time: Sports activities, hobbies, associations and honorary offices etc.

Become Aware Of Your Achievements

Start utilizing your biography as a resource by becoming aware of your achievements. We often easily remember our "failures" and our achievements remain in the shadows – unless we take a closer look and actively make ourselves aware of them.

Take a look at your biography and reflect upon these questions: What have you achieved in your life? What kind of accomplishments have you obtained? What went well, where were you outstandingly successful? Where did you secure a victory? But also: What kind of challenging situations did you conquer? What kind of tasks did you fulfill? What did you master? And: How did you handle setbacks? Did you get up, dust off your shoulders and kept walking or were you discouraged and stayed on the floor? Even in the way you handled so-called "failures" or "defeats", personal qualities can become transparent. Remove the label "failure" and ask yourself: "Who am I that I have made it through this? What are the characteristics and qualities I obviously have if I was able to overcome this?"

For many people, this is a very empowering and encouraging step which often has a direct effect on their self-esteem and self-confidence.

Who Have You Become In The Process?

In the next step, you take a closer look at your accomplishments and examine them in terms of - possibly hidden - qualities, competencies and special characteristics that made them possible. Start by exactly describing each accomplishment in three steps:

1. *Situation*:

What exactly was the situation? What was the problem? What was the task or the challenge? Be as detailed in your description of the situation as possible.

2. *Action*:

What did you do to conquer the situation? How did you solve the problem? What was your contribution in dealing with this challenge? Describe your approach in all sub-steps and as detailed as possible.

3. *Result:*
What was the ultimate outcome, the result? Describe how the situation changed through your action.

Once you have put down this detailed description, zoom in and think about these questions: "If I have resolved this situation in such and such manner, if I was able to accomplish that – then what am I obviously capable of? What am I apparently really good at? What kind of competencies and qualities do I obviously possess that made me so successful?"

Recognize Your Qualities

Now it gets really exciting: Your personal competencies become visible. There will be some you were already aware of and that simply get confirmed. Then, there will be some you recognize for the first time. To many, this step is an unfamiliar and sometimes difficult one because in many cases, personal qualities are perceived as something natural and not as special strengths, leading to a so-called "strength blindness". In fact, it is because you are especially good at something that you yourself may not consider it as something special.

"He that praises himself spatters himself!" – Who has not heard this proverb which aims at making sure we don't push ourselves and our qualities to the fore. The intention behind this attitude obviously is to avoid self-exaltation and arrogance. Unfortunately though, in many cases it leads people towards the other extreme. They hide their light under a bushel and humble themselves to avoid standing out.

Both attitudes can be a hindrance in the process of recognizing your true qualities. To avoid this effect, you can try to consciously take on an observer's position. Take on an external perspective and think about this: "Let's assume someone else would have resolved the situation the same way, would have done the same thing and attained the same result. What kind of competencies and qualities would I attribute to this person?" If this approach is still too ambitious or just won't work, then go ahead and actually let someone else assess the situation together with you.

Self-Perception And Perception By Others: The Blind Spots

Self-reflection is important, but can only take us to a certain point: Our "blind spots". You can compare this phenomenon to driving, where you also have a blind spot in your rear view mirror. It is the area in which there is something that you cannot see, but that can be seen by others. Everyone in your environment can see: There is a car behind you, getting ready to pass you and if you now decide to pull over to the other lane, there will be a crash. We have blind spots in our behavior, in our effect on others, in what we do, in how we express our personality.

There are aspects of our behavior and our impact, that other people in our environment notice, but that we are unaware of. The goal is to reduce these blind spots; ideally to the point where you have a comprehensive self-image which is congruent with the perception of others.

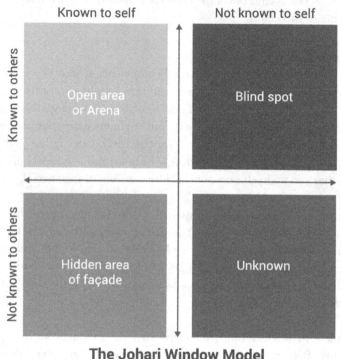

The Johari Window Model
Image 5: Blind Spot

This means that self-exploration should not be limited to navel-gazing in the sense of contemplation and examination of oneself. Moreover, it should integrate the views and perception of others since after all, how others see you is just as much part of reality as your perception. You should have a viable understanding of how others perceive you – in different situations, in various social systems. In this process of self-exploration, it may be helpful to obtain feedback from others. Ask people you trust to provide you with an assessment of your qualities and your limitations, ask them to describe situations in which those become visible. Obtain feedback from your professional or your personal environment, or from both. Then proceed to compare the results with your self-image and clarify larger differences in a dialogue.

Preferences And Aversions

Another helpful question in in the critical assessment of yourself is the question regarding your preferences and aversions. Again, starting with your biography. What do you enjoy doing? Wherein lies your passion? When are you easily able to stay focused over an extended period of time? What do you not enjoy? What drains your energy?

When you look at all of the above in its essence, you see your personal self-concept: Wherein lie your true strengths? What are you really good at? What distinguishes you? What do you thoroughly enjoy doing? Therewith you receive the answers to the first two questions of the Ikigai model: What are you good at and what do you enjoy doing?

The self-concept you gain in this process brings several advantages:

// Becoming aware of your achievements, abilities and characteristics has an encouraging effect.
// It enables you to better communicate and clearly illustrate the mentioned factors. This is of great importance, particularly when it comes to professional reorientation. The clearer your understanding is of what you stand for and who you are, the clearer you are able to communicate that in the course of a hiring process – verbally and in writing.

When you have done the preparatory work and are ready to give examples of situations in which you have proven one quality or another based on having carefully examined your achievements and if, on top of that, you are able to demonstrate that you have learned to handle your limitations, then you will be able to earn significant extra credit in the hiring process.

Values And Belief Systems

Values are like guard rails that ensure we stay on track when we follow our visions and objectives. Most of the time, our own set of values remains subconscious. However, it continuously influences our thinking, our perception of what is right and what is wrong – and ultimately our behavior and actions. It allows us to evaluate whether our objectives are in line with our integrity. Let's assume I was to wake you up at two-thirty in the morning and ask you: "What are the three most important values in your life?" Apart from one of the answers at that moment probably being "sleep", only few people would be able to provide a clear answer to that question.

There is a difference between philosophical values and practiced values. Philosophical values are those we deem important, but are not extraordinarily committed to. A good example of a philosophical value is world peace. You may believe world peace to be very important and support it, but you may not necessarily invest time, money or energy to live this value. In contrast, there are practiced values, values we are willing to invest in – time, money or energy. A typical practiced value could be health. You invest time, energy and possibly money to do sports, eat healthy and do something good for your body.

The term belief system in this context describes our inner convictions and thought patterns which evolve from all our experiences. We form many beliefs based on what was instilled in us in our upbringing. This means we adopted them at some point from important attachment figures. They are not always helpful or beneficial for us at a later point in life. In fact, they may even be a hindrance in our development.

So take a moment to sit down and write down all core beliefs that come to mind when you think about various subjects of life: Profession and career, money, relationships, health and fitness, family, personal development etc. Then take each of those beliefs and ask yourself: Is this really true? Do I agree with that? Do I believe in this or did I simply adopt this belief? Which part of this do I believe to be right, which part do I actually believe to be wrong? In what area of my life and how does this belief currently influence me in my life? Where and how is it conducive and where is it possibly a hindrance in my development, in achieving my goals? Sometimes, it makes sense to throw a belief over board if you come to the conclusion that it hinders you more than support you in attaining your objectives.

Basic Needs

In evolutionary terms, we humans are mainly driven by substances in the brain which manifest themselves in various fundamental needs. These human needs have been described by many experts in the most diverse ways. The probably most well-known model is the hierarchy of needs pyramid described by Maslow[5]. His theory states that humans progressively fulfill needs according to their hierarchical levels. He assumed that we only reach higher levels of needs once our basic needs have been met – in this case the need for security and safety. At the top of the pyramid, he put self-fulfillment, which includes spiritual development and growth, for instance.

However, from a neuroscientific perspective, this model has been overtaken. Our brain and our organism do not function hierarchically. Otherwise, cultures who live in poverty would not have any spiritual rituals or convictions – which they often do have. Especially in difficult or even threatening circumstances, the need for spirituality can be very strong, which directly contradicts Maslow's theory. In fact, our brain operates on all levels simultaneously. We only develop a certain hierarchy in case of extreme needs and imminent danger, such as when we are about to be attacked by a sable-toothed tiger and fall into fight or flight mode and no longer think about food, sexual fulfillment or spiritual development.

Hence, I refer to a model which was developed by my colleague Andy Habermacher[6], who in turn refers to the work of Klaus Grawe. Grawe's paper in the area of neuropsychotherapy illustrates four core human needs which all human beings have in common, independent of age, time and cultural context. Habermacher, Ghadiri and Peters refined Grawe's theory into their SCOAP theory, which additionally considers historical aspects and encompasses five needs that correspond to the evolutionary development of the brain. These are:

// *Self-esteem:* Maintaining and increasing self-esteem; gaining appreciation;
// *Control:* Having control over the environment; having autonomy and freedom;
// *Orientation:* Understanding the environment; knowing what needs to be done;
// *Attachment:* Having an attachment figure and social relationships;
// *Pleasure:* Increasing enjoyment and satisfaction; avoiding any negative.

The simple basic assumption is that human beings are always driven by these core needs and that they form the biggest and most fundamental drivers. How they manifest themselves may differ depending on personality, culture and development. Some people are driven more by their need for self-esteem, others place more importance on attachment.

Understanding these core needs allows us to improve in getting in touch with our inner drivers. It enables us to better understand how our rational thinking revolves around fulfilling those needs. Maybe we decide to study at a university in order to find a better job (self-esteem), be able to lead a more interesting life (pleasure), have more financial resources (control), obtain relevant knowledge (orientation) and possibly find a partner with similar interests (attachment).
Fulfilling our needs is enriching and leads to motivation patterns. Disregarding or violating our needs leads to stress reactions, can be destructive and lead to demotivation.

Approach And Avoidance

All organisms develop an approach motivation, e.g. to nutrition, and an avoidance motivation, e.g. away from danger. Both are instinctive reflexes and emotional drivers in the brain and biology of all living creatures. So, we can distinguish two kinds of motivation:

Approach: to move closer to something, get near, reach
Avoidance: to stay away from something, withdraw, defensive

Both approaches are natural and we bear both within us. We look left and right before crossing a street. We are careful about whom we entrust our money and avoid dangerous situations just as much as we seek things that are beneficial to us or our situation. But the most important fact is that some people are driven more by avoidance strategies and others more by approach strategies. One person is more prone to reacting to positive impulses, the other more to negative ones. What motivates us differs and what attracts one person may repel another. Therefore, it is important that we understand and recognize our needs and the needs of others so that we can be more effective in dealing with ourselves and others.

Discover Your Potential

Ultimately, self-exploration is all about gaining a comprehensive self-image. The clearer it is, the better you can look outwards and see opportunities for you to contribute, identify where you fit in in terms of company, position, function or role – or recognize where you do not fit in and what doesn't suit you.

Thankfully, we are living in a time which allows us to re-invent ourselves once, twice or even several times over the course of a professional career, completely reposition ourselves and do whatever our heart desires. I often coach clients who reach a point where they ask themselves: "What am I doing here, particularly in terms of my profession? And is this what I truly want? Is it what I am truly best at? Am I following my passion or could there be another road I could take?" Not always, but in many cases those questions appear central around the middle age.

The process they enter can be compared to that of a snake shedding its skin – realizing it has outgrown it and starting to get rid of it. In this sense, this process is a process of discovery. It is not about adding to the person you already are because there might be something missing. Instead, it is about discovering, unveiling and exposing what is already there – the potential, qualities, competencies, passion for what wants to be lived and brought into the light in order to unfold.

"Perfection is finally attained not when there is

**no longer anything to add, but when there is
no longer anything to take away."**
ANTOINE DE ST. EXUPÉRY[7]

This process of discovery is mainly about removing the rubble and blowing off the dust; rubble and dust that came from our conditioning and socialization, our closely knit web of beliefs, values, opinions and attitudes which we adopted from our parents and other influencers and further developed on our own over the course of time.

Making yourself aware of this old skin of conditioning and letting go of what no longer fits: This requires you recognizing and acknowledging yourself. There is something very liberating about beginning to realize just how amazing you are. When you begin to realize that you are not the little I, the little self you long believed you were. Basically, it is not any different from getting to know another person. Through the intensive confrontation with yourself, a relationship develops which is shaped by understanding and a favorable attitude.

In a forest monastery in Vietnam, there stood a large Buddha statue made from clay, which was regularly cared for and cleaned by the monks who lived there. Over the years, the cleaning work created small cracks in the clay – and through these cracks, a golden gleam started to appear. The monks got curious and removed the clay. What they discovered took their breath away: Underneath the clay surface, they found a golden Buddha statue that had been hidden under the clay by their predecessors during the turmoil of war so that it would not fall into the hands of their enemies.

Often, the same applies to us human beings: Behind the walls of self-protection and self-sustainment which we have built up over the years, lies the golden core that characterizes us and that we have preserved from our childhood. Strive to bring this true essence to light and start with exploring and rediscovering for yourself who you really are.

Where Do You Want To Go?

In the third and last step, the insight you have gained helps in taking a look ahead. You can apply this step to various areas of your life, depending on what is relevant and therefore makes sense to you. Maybe you already have a good sense of what it could be like when everything comes together and feels right. When you have found and are living your personal Ikigai. It is less a matter of defining specific objectives, but rather about describing the quality you wish to have in your life.

Be reminded: The objective is to optimally express who you are, with your potential, and to contribute to a greater good. In order to illustrate this, I like making the following comparison: Imagine yourself being a plant. Maybe an oak tree, a pine tree or a beautiful orchid. All of the potential is already contained in the plant's seed. Bringing it to its fruition is only a matter of creating the right environment: An orchid needs the right soil, it needs water, the right temperature, the right amount of sun – not too much, not too little. Then it will turn out to be what it can be. It will not turn into an oak tree, no matter how badly it wants to develop it into one.

If you put an orchid into an inadequate environment, maybe in the ideal environment for an oak tree, it may only turn into an underdeveloped orchid. All because it continues to feel like it should be an oak tree among other oak trees, trying really hard to become one – and missing the opportunity to become the orchid it could have become. And because maybe it continues to overhear that it isn't or may never become a good oak tree, you can't be surprised if it never reaches its full bloom.

> **"If you judge a fish by its ability to climb a tree,**
> **it will live its whole life believing it is stupid."**
> (OFTEN ATTRIBUTED TO ALBERT EINSTEIN)

Or to put it differently: The better you know what kind of plant you are, what characterizes you and what kind of conditions you need to blossom, the better you are able to choose the environment you should put yourself in.

SELF-AWARENESS
///

This section basically deals with a form of self-exploration as well, however, it does so in a different, more holistic way. Here, we address gaining access to the lower parts of the iceberg, those parts that do not necessarily present themselves by way of rational thinking, but by other means. I am particularly referring to becoming aware of your thought patterns, emotions, inner reactions and impulses through observation. Those can be accessed mainly by becoming more attentive to your perceptions and directing your attention. So, contrary to the last section, we now talk about self-perception rather than rational self-exploration.

The Storyteller

For most of us, thought processes, to a great extent, occur without our conscious control. Still, our thinking significantly impacts our happiness, so it can be very helpful to become more aware of your thoughts. A Harvard University study conducted in 2010[8] examined the correlation between mind wandering and a happy, content attitude towards life. The study shows that the way we think has greater influence on our happiness than what we do. It also showed that apparently, people are less happy and content when they let their mind wander than when they are engaged in their current task, focused and present in the here and now. The core finding of the two Harvard professors Matthew A. Killingsworth and Daniel T. Gilbert subsequently was: "A wandering mind is an unhappy mind."

> ## "The rational mind is a good servant, but a poor master."
> ALBERT EINSTEIN

Obviously, there is nothing wrong with intelligent and targeted thinking. Our rational mind is an excellent tool we can use to solve complex problems and fulfill tasks. What I am referring to here is more a matter of automated thinking in autopilot mode. The term "monkey mind" aptly describes the nature of the uncontrolled mind: When the rational mind is not controlled, it does exactly what it is supposed to do. It produces thoughts. Just like it is a hair root's job to grow hair, or the salivary glands' to produce saliva, it produces comments and stories on what we experience within ourselves and within our environment.

For many people, this self-contained thinking causes a significant "thought noise" that usually starts with the first thoughts in the morning, only a few seconds after waking up: "What day is today? Tuesday? Oh no, the meeting with my boss at 10 o'clock…. that is going to be a challenge…". Then, one thought follows the other. By the time you are in the shower, figuratively speaking, the boss and half of your colleagues are right there with you, plus all upcoming meetings, emails and tasks awaiting you that day. This creates several thousand individual thoughts per day. In the worst case, our own thinking keeps us from falling asleep at night because our rational mind simply will not stop thinking.

Besides, the bigger part of this automated thinking is repetitive. Old thoughts, familiar thought patterns. The same as last week, the same stories as last year. At the same time, our mind has a tendency to evaluate everything. It actually is a thinking and evaluating machine. It continuously assesses and evaluates what happens to us – on the inside and on the outside: Good, bad, I like it, I don't like it, how can he say something like that, what is wrong with him. We constantly label everything we experience. We judge, and in the worst case, we even condemn. This continuous judging forces us into acting in a reactive manner without thinking and usually not even being aware of it. Compare this to a television set which runs all day and shows a subtitle or comment sent from the "off", telling us a story about every single image we see.

The core problem is that this inner storyteller exerts an almost magical attraction on our attention and we tend not only to listen to it but also to identify with it, or even get lost in it. This leads to us often entering a state of "being lost in thought" or "absorbed in thought" – and thus little aware of the moment. We drive our car in that state of mind or cross a busy road as a pedestrian, perhaps even holding our smartphone in our hand. Even in conversations we are often not fully present because we tend to immediately follow each inner thought and let it distract us from our conversation. This has even turned into a social phenomenon for which the American author Linda Stone[9] has found a term: Continuous Partial Attention (CPA).

Inner Weather

Likewise, you can picture your ever-present emotional movements as "inner weather", inner weather phenomena that emerge and disappear again. Similar to the weather outside, they are always in motion. Continually changing temperatures fluctuate, sometimes the sky is steel-blue and calm. Then clouds appear, wind comes along, first a warm breeze, the clouds become thicker, the sky gets darker, a thunderstorm is rolling in, we get caught in a torrential downpour, lightning, thunder ... and then it stops. The air is clear again, the clouds move on and the sun reappears. It is all a matter of developing an awareness for what your inner weather looks like and what kind of climate there is.

My British colleague, John Parr[10], an expert for emotional intelligence whom I have learned a lot from about effective human interaction, describes this as follows: "The body uses an electrochemical communication system, and emotions are experienced when chemicals, build up and are then be reabsorbed again. This process is not 'binary', i.e. on and off, but is 'analogue' taking time to grow and dissipate. When our calm is 'disturbed' we become aroused, the electrochemical process begins. If we recognize the associated 'feeling' as information relating to a change in the environment that requires our attention, then the emotional charge will provide motivation to solve the problem. When the problem is resolved, the process will be reversed and the chemicals reabsorbed. Depending upon our perception of the magnitude of the problem and the time taken to solve the problem, these chemical reactions ebb and flow to greater or lesser degrees and time periods. Therefore, I see emotions being experienced in waves and not as pulses."

The half-life of emotions is relatively short. Usually they disappear within minutes, if they are not additionally fueled. That means an emotion arises, develops and grows. Now if you do not nurture this emotion, adding oil to the fire, so to speak, with the stories you tell yourself about the emotion, if instead, you simply allow the emotion to exist and accept it for what it is, refraining from resisting of fighting it, then it often disappears all on its own.

Let's take a simple example: You come back from a meeting and you are upset about how it went. Instead of simply accepting that and thereby allowing it to disappear, you start telling yourself stories about it. "How could he make such a comment? Who does he think he is? That was typical for him! He always does that in those meeting when I am there! And he does that in front of others! Dismisses me just like that! That is so disrespectful and inacceptable!"… I am sure, you know this or similar kinds of inner dialogue from your own experience. This will not calm your inner thunderstorm. Therefore, distraction can be a helpful strategy: by focusing directly on a rational brain challenge, e.g. a mathematical task, and activating brain areas which are in charge of your rational thinking.

The Survival Radar

The evaluating and judgmental nature of our rational mind is compounded by the fact that in our perception, we are not realistic but subject to a strong negative distortion. In psychology, this phenomenon is called "negativity bias": things our rational mind labels as "negative" attract our attention like a magnet. At the same time, we seem to have a non-stick coating for the many positive things and are thus forced to consciously take a close look in order to notice them at all.

"A falling tree makes more noise than a growing forest."
ASIAN PROVERB

It is as if we look at anything supposedly negative through a magnifying glass while anything positive appears small and insignificant. This is a completely natural distortion of perception we go through life with. That is totally fine because it has a lot to do with survival and has been deeply rooted within us throughout the ages. When our predecessors who were still living in caves went out hunting, they had to turn their inner radar to anything negative and potentially threatening. We still carry that within us, even though in our civilization, we usually no longer experience life-threatening situations.

This "survival mode" is practically the standard calibration of our brain which is programmed to ensuring our survival and thus constantly preoccupied with identifying and resolving problems. We are permanently in problem solving mode. In order to survive that is important and right. It just unfortunately leads to our storyteller often being in a bad mood and, with his stories and evaluations, presenting reality to us in a distorted way.

I am sure you know your inner critic who gets especially loud and provides you with his comments when you feel you were unsuccessful at something. Those comments and inner dialogues which partially originate from your childhood and still express themselves in adulthood: "You are running late again, you are not worthy, you are not valuable enough, you can't do this anyway, you messed up again, this is typical for you ..."

Four Steps To Attain Greater Mindfulness

Terms like mindfulness or presence have become increasingly popular in recent years and point the way towards better quality of life through improved self-awareness and self-control. This clearly shows that there is an increasing awareness in society for the importance of those factors. Basically, these ideas are not based on new findings but rather millennia-old traditions. Thankfully, the increasing scientific progress of the last decades, helped that the positive effects of these practices on well-being and health could be proven and confirmed through brain research.

I started learning more about techniques of systematic deep relaxation and mindfulness meditation at the age of 18. A program called MBSR[11], which is well-suited for our western cultural context was developed by the US-American Jon Kabat-Zinn[12]. The highly efficient and easily accessible program has thus found its way into many companies. Basically, it is similar to visiting a fitness studio or a gym: you go there to increase your overall fitness so you are better prepared for meeting life's challenges. Of course, there can be other motives as well, but I am not focusing on those at the moment. Perhaps you exercise with weights to strengthen specific muscle groups, preventing back pain, for example, or you train your overall fitness to increase your physical resilience.

Nevertheless, what are you doing for your mental and emotional fitness? How do you train your rational mind, the conscious control of your perception? Unfortunately, there aren't any fitness centers for the brain yet. But with the following four steps, you will be able to develop more mindfulness, and with that comes more mental and emotional fitness. You can do this on your own and at any given time. Do you remember the iceberg? When you train your attentiveness, you increase the permeability between the conscious and the unconscious shares of your personality by lowering the awareness threshold. In brief: You are in better contact with yourself.

Step One: Recognition

Any change starts with the conscious perception and discovery of that which is, the current situation and the current state. This means you first have to become aware of your storyteller and your inner weather, because it isn't until you sharpen your self-perception that you will be able to recognize what it is that you are thinking all day long. How you react to things that happen to you – not only the things that actually do happen, but also and foremost to your own thoughts and emotions.

This requires taking on a neutral observant position in order to allow yourself to become aware of your habits regarding your thinking, judging and feeling as well as their effects on your behavior. Mindfulness develops when you start paying close attention to those processes. As if someone was kindly asking what was going on at the moment. It may be helpful to use visualization, especially in the beginning. Here are some examples which have proven to work:

// Picture your stream of thoughts as a busy road. Each thought is a car driving by. Now sit down at the side of the road and observe what kind of thoughts come closer and disappear again. You don't have to actually get in each car and ride along.

// The often used term "train of thoughts" displays another helpful idea: You can get off and watch the trains go by.

// Or you picture your thoughts as clouds in the sky. They build up, pass by, and dissolve again. You will soon realize that thoughts also dissolve when you don't pursue them and instead allow them to simply pass by.

// Imagine your thoughts like a flowing river: Sit down by the riverside and watch from the outside for a change, instead of always trying not to drown in it, or even fighting it and swimming against the current.

// And if you liked the image of the television set mentioned earlier: Leave the set, take a seat of a spectator and watch from the outside what kind of program is currently showing.

With a little practice you will reach a point where you yourself decide if you want to go along with your thoughts or if you would rather opt out and let them run in the background. You then no longer inevitably follow every thought and thereby gain a certain inner distance. It is not about brining all thoughts to a standstill or switching off your rational mind when you don't need it, that isn't necessary at all.

It is only a matter of becoming an observer of your own thinking, gaining more space among the high density of thoughts and taking a step back.

Handling this process in an attentive manner is as if we were to switch on the light in a dark room and allow the light to shine upon everything, which then suddenly appears clearly in front of us, simply to detect it, without assessing or evaluating it. It may be helpful to call our perception: "I see, worries." "I see, happiness!" "Hmm, conflicts." "Tension – interesting ..." And: "Here I go again, assessing and judging." It is as if you were to expose the iceberg by lowering the waterline and thus the threshold of awareness. This form of recognition takes you from unconsciousness and autopilot mode to consciousness and freedom of choice in the driver seat.

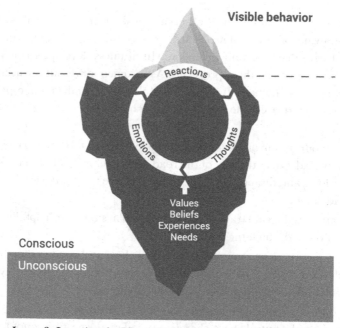

Image 6: Lowering the Threshold of Awareness through Mindfulness

When you realize and experience for yourself that you are able to simply turn down the volume of your rational mind and allow it to only run in the background, there is something very liberating about that. Take on a curious-neutral position and avoid any kind of resistance against your thinking or a certain kind of thought.

The same is true for your emotions, your inner weather. Picture yourself as a huge, stable, calm mountain which is surrounded by continuously and naturally changing weather. That has a completely different feel to it than feeling like a leaf of a tree, totally exposed to the wind. Accept the weather for what it is and simply observe. Become an observer and witness of your inner world.

Step Two: Acceptance

Once you realize the nature of the rational mind and that it is primarily a storyteller who spends all day doing nothing but sitting in your head and commenting everything you experience, then it will become easier for you to accept it for what it is. The rational mind is only doing its job. Moreover, once you realize that you will only feed and strengthen it when offering resistance, it will become easier for you not to try to stop it. Ideally, you will reach a point where you take on an inner attitude of simply allowing it to talk. Particularly your inner critic. Particularly the worries which tend to think so highly of themselves, coming along with big, shiny banners saying "Take me seriously, you need to worry now about that meeting tomorrow! This is essential! It matters now! You are not supposed to sleep!"

The initial inner reflex usually is the desire to hush or get rid of those kinds of thoughts. "I don't want that now, I don't want to be worried. This makes me uncomfortable and it needs to stop. I need to get to sleep!" Unpleasant feelings are triggered and you try to fight them. Or we seek distraction and numb ourselves. Many of our actions do not lead to the desired results, but first and foremost serve the purpose of distracting us from what is unpleasant – or, more precisely: to distract us from ourselves. Constantly checking our smartphone, checking our tablet, starring at the numbing TV – often that is nothing more than a diversion. We may even actually anesthetize ourselves with alcohol or other substances in an attempt to silence the hum of thoughts. In doing so, we avoid welcoming what lies underneath, our own thinking and feeling, in an appreciative and openly accepting way.

The problem is that we are unable to be selective in numbing ourselves. We can't just erase the "bad" thoughts and feelings. When we choose to numb ourselves – in whatever way – we do it collectively. This means the emotions we generally deem "positive" are affected as well – which deprives us of our liveliness. However, the way out of uncomfortable thoughts and feelings does not take us via resistance and wanting to remove them – instead, it leads us straight through them. There is no shortcut. Only by accepting and appreciating our thoughts and emotions we can live through and thereby overcome them.

**"The highest level of wisdom is
to simply let matters take their course."**
CONFUCIUS

Therefore, this second step is about embracing and making friends with your storyteller and accepting the inner weather. Nobody would think of rising up against the weather and saying. "This must not happen! It cannot rain now!", even though a lot of people tend to comment and evaluate the weather. The stunning effect usually is that while the storyteller may not be completely silenced, it will become more quiet. Thanks to you developing a sympathetic, accepting relationship with it, it no longer has to be so loud and show off. Rather, it continues to do what it needs to do – just in a more restrained and discrete manner.

The same is true for external events. Start by generally accepting whatever happens to you – after all, it already is a fact anyway. My friend and MBSR trainer Jeannine Born[13] explains that acceptance is neither passive nor naive. According to her, acceptance is an active decision to start by entering into contact with a situation, even when it is challenging, and feel the emotions that are there. She believes that this creates a different kind of basis for making decisions with a clear mind and not driven by fear and preconceptions. She goes on to explain that conscious acting, or not acting because there is nothing to be done, then becomes possible in the space which we create for ourselves to be able to consciously choose, and when we learn to consider each moment, each event, every situation as something complete and we allow ourselves to accept it the way it is.

Acceptance is not about resignation, either. It is not about simply accepting everything and surrendering to life – at least not in the sense of drifting away without any intentions and not wanting to change anything in life any more. If you are unhappy with your circumstances, acceptance does not mean that you don't change them. Acceptance merely means that you simply understand what is already there and work with that instead of remaining tense and reactive in your resistance against it.

So, should you happen to be on a plane sitting next to someone with a strong body odor, or if there is a child two rows in front of you screaming blue murder, you may initially get upset about it. However, if you take a closer look at your reaction, then you will often realize that it is your own resistance against the odor or the screaming that drives you crazy. Once you are able to simply allow what is happening to exist – the child is screaming, that's the reality of the moment – you can deal with the issue in a completely different way. You may even develop compassion for the child and the parents. And you can still try to find a different seat. It doesn't mean that you have to endure the next ten hours in this position if that poses a problem. Likewise, there are many other examples for situations in which you may not approve of what is going on. Start by accepting it and then ask yourself: What does this situation require and what can be done?

In a sense, acceptance allows us to relax and become open to the facts in front of us. This second step is important because the recognition (step 1) naturally may cause feelings of rejection or resistance and the wish that things may be different. Hence, acceptance does not mean that we can't work on improving things. It only means that, for the time being, things are the way they are.

"Life is difficult." is the first sentence of the book *"The Road Less Traveled"* written by M. Scott Peck[14]. This shows that it is fundamental to recognize and accept that life naturally is full of challenges and difficulties. That it consists of natural wave movements, just like the ones that can be found all over nature. Joy is followed by grief, happiness is followed by pain – on various levels. Based on this form of acceptance and respect, problems which seem unmanageable, often become more tangible and thus easier to resolve.

While during the first step, recognition, we realize that we are swimming with the tide of our stream of thoughts, what happens in the second step – acceptance – can be described as follows: We stop swimming against the tide. We realize that we are fighting against something that is real. We try to swim in the opposite direction, against the tide of life's circumstances. So, acceptance is the prerequisite for letting go and the opposite of holding on. If someone is unable to fall asleep, that person can't let go in a way, because sleep is our natural way of practicing the art of letting go on a daily basis. Often accepting the fact that we can't sleep is what leads to us being able to do just that: fall asleep.

In the second step, we say "yes" to the moment as it is. Alone by doing so, usually a feeling of relaxation and ease concerning the initial emotion kicks in. And if you are unable to accept a moment for what it is, then accept just that: The fact that you don't succeed in doing so at the moment.

Step Three: Investigation

Recognition and acceptance lead to the third step: Investigating and understanding the reasons why we react the way we react. Why we feel the way we do. Why we think the way we think. That is, why we sometimes choose to swim against the tide.

In order to better understand why something is the way it is, we take a closer look at these three aspects: Our reactions, thoughts, and emotions. They all first manifest themselves in our body. That means, when you find yourself confronted with a difficult situation, you can take the following approach to gain a better understanding of what is happening: Use your perception of your body to determine where the issue manifests itself. Maybe you can sense heat somewhere in your body, tension, stiffness, vibration. Maybe you experience numbness or a certain kind of tingling. You can go on and investigate how you react to this bodily sensation. With acceptance or resistance?

How does your perception of your bodily sensations change when you simply perceive them in an open and accepting way? Do you open up? Are there possibly several layers of perception? Is there a center? Does the sensation become stronger? Does it change? Does it move? Does it reoccur? Or does it resolve itself already simply due to you giving it your attention?

What kind of emotions are linked with this challenge? Is the primary feeling pleasant, unpleasant, or neutral? Are you attentive to this feeling? What other feelings come with this emotion? When taking a mindful approach, each feeling receives the same level of attention and recognition. We examine how each emotion feels, whether it is pleasant, painful, tense, relaxed or sad. We try to localize the emotion in our body: Where can you feel it most intensely and what happens once you encounter it in a mindful way?

Next, we explore the movements that take place in our rational mind in the situation we are confronted with. What kind of thoughts or images do you associate with this challenge? What kind of stories do you tell yourself about this situation? What kind of assessments, evaluations, convictions, and beliefs do you bear within you?

Once you take a closer look, you will often realize that some of these emotions, convictions, thoughts or stories are fixed beliefs of ideas – or outdated perspectives based on habits. You will recognize that they are merely stories you tell yourself about the situation, and you will realize that you do not have to believe them.

Step Four: Non-Identification

In this last step, you direct your attention to the fact that you ARE not your thoughts and emotions, but you HAVE thoughts and emotions. Non-identification means that your self-identity is not defined by your thinking and feeling. This leads to a natural feeling of freedom and ease. You simply let go of identifying with your thoughts and emotions.

You are not the storyteller and you are not the inner weather, either. In this step, you cease to perceive inner and outer experiences as "I" or "mine". You recognize how identifying with how you think, feel, and experience a situation leads to subordination, fear, and a lack of authenticity. Using the image of the river, letting go and refraining from identifying with your thoughts, feelings and actions is the last step, it means getting out of the river: You understand that you are not the river. Instead, you take a seat by the riverside and watch. This ability to let go of your intellectual thinking, of habitual thoughts, and letting go of emotions and reactions poses a fundamental finding which, for many people, comes with a great gain of personal freedom. It is like flying: By taking off you put some distance between what is going on around you and yourself – and allow yourself to look at things from a new perspective and thus see the bigger picture from a bird's eye view.

This process of developing awareness is not only one in which awareness becomes separated from thoughts. It is also a process during which the assessment and evaluation starts to become detached from the actual situations and issues and in which the situations and their evaluation is being perceived as two different aspects. There is a fundamental difference between a real problem and one that you imagine, think about and fear that it may become reality. In a letter he wrote to a friend towards the end of his life, the French philosopher and mathematician René Descartes[15] stated: "My life has been full of mishaps, most of which never happened."

A higher level of self-awareness is the key to any change, because we can only control what we are aware of. What we are not aware of controls us.

SELF-MANAGEMENT
//

In this section, I intentionally choose not to talk about the common self- and time-management techniques and methods. Many other books describe tools such as the Eisenhower Matrix which serves to help set priorities according to a certain system, or the Pareto principle which intends to increase efficiency. These and many other techniques I find important and helpful. However, they often fall short when other important aspects of good self-management are neglected. Therefore, I will focus on other aspects.

Are You A Human Being Or A Human Doing?
In most areas of our lives, balance is of great importance. Nature is literally a living example: Seasons change, there is day and night, tides come and go. Wherever humans have not caused imbalances, everything is in a state of natural duality in which, in so many cases, two poles create a whole only based on the balance between them. Our health depends on it, so does our happiness with ourselves and with others. The same is true for the balance between being and doing, between active and passive mode, between Yin and Yang. However, often

the balance is missing: There is an imbalance to the advantage of doing and the disadvantage of being, silence, and mere existence. This is particularly true for the work environment and, in many ways, for the way many people spend their leisure time. When was the last time you didn't do anything? Really nothing at all?

We are "human *beings*", not "human *doings*". This means we should not define ourselves only by what we do, but also by what we are. Primarily, we *are* humans. For this reason, we have to attain equilibrium between doing and being. For most of us, this does not mean we should do even more, but learn how to simply be. When I say "be", I do not mean taking a break at work to check your Facebook or Instagram account. Nor do I mean going home and spending your evening numbing yourself in front of the TV. With "being", I mean a relaxed presence in everything that is – on the outside and on the inside. Including noise and other sensory perceptions, the inner life and its thoughts and emotions. Simply doing nothing and entering a state of silence, to truly only be. Compare this process to a glass of dirty water. If you keep stirring it, the water remains murky. In order to regain a clear view, you have to leave things alone so that the impurities can settle.

Our active mode not only becomes visible through external activity. Just as often, it is expressed in our inner actions and thus in the previously described automatic and uncontrolled thinking. Attentiveness is the tool of choice when it comes to transitioning from doing into being. Doing sports can serve the same purpose. What matters when doing sports is whether the movement is driven by performance orientation or serves the purpose of relaxation. Insofar, there are two kinds of approaches to reaching balance and relaxation from doing: Active and passive. Both are important, both are right. It is, however, imperative to create the right balance between active and passive. The passive form of recovery in the form of sleep, relaxation techniques or meditation is especially helpful when an area in our life requires high concentration. Creating greater equilibrium has proven to directly affect our thinking: A brain which has the opportunity to retreat to a quiet state of being, "idle", so to speak, becomes ultimately more efficient.

I have attended retreats on various occasions, for example at the Lassalle-Haus in Menzingen, Switzerland. This place offers short retreats which usually take place from Friday until Sunday night. Such retreats offer the advantage of providing room for silence – not only in a physical sense, but also in terms of the time silence requires. What makes these retreats even more exciting is that the participants spend all three days in complete silence, internally and externally. As far as times reserved for meditation are concerned, this is obviously not very challenging to comply with. But once thirty people are having lunch together and nobody says a word, this turns into an unusual situation – which gains a very special quality thanks to the silence.

Once the noise of people talking is missing, the room for perception automatically increases, which then allows for all senses to become open and perceptive: The taste of the food, the smells, the sounds that are created when people share a meal. This is augmented by the presence of your own thoughts, which is thereby increased – something that is not necessarily only pleasant. I can highly recommend such a retreat if you would like to experience this kind of counterbalance in a highly intense way.

Following an experience like that, the next step is integrating silence into daily life and slipping in short moments of attentive being into your routine. This could be in the form of taking two or three conscious breaths, or a consciously chosen presence and attentiveness for what you are doing at the moment: When you wash your hands, be there, completely. Perceive the smell of the soap, feel the water on your hands and just be there, be with what you are doing. You can also consciously focus on your breath, the noise that surrounds you, or the emotions that emerge in you.

In other words: Take your foot off the gas pedal and put yourself in idle. Or, if you want to take your smartphones route: Change into flight mode, every now and then.

Create Room For Choice

Who doesn't know this setting: Your work day is filled to the brim with tasks, phone calls, appointments, meetings. One thing leads to another, one problem is barely solved and immediately followed by another. Everyone needs something from us. And, as if that were not enough, after hours, the program continues with after-work networking, a fitness center visit, picking up children etc. Days are packed so fully, it almost becomes impossible to bear it all. Those kinds of days build up into a series of weeks which are only interrupted by weekends just as packed and lead to months just flying by in time lapse. And before you know it, a new year has begun. So often we are driven, constantly reacting and controlled by others. What can we do?

Well, this actually is the wrong question. It is not about doing yet something else, only increasing the density of tasks. Instead, the attention needs to be directed towards something which nowadays, usually gets neglected, and then this attention needs to slowly be increased: Space. Space as the opposite of internal and external density you feel. As long as you do not create space, you cannot make a conscious choice – whether it is the choice of where you want to direct your attention or how you would like to respond to an external event. Without space, you remain unconscious and reactive instead of conscious and pro-active.

> **"Between stimulus and response, there is a space.
> In that space is our power to choose our response."**
> VIKTOR E. FRANKL[16]

Creating External Space

The more we believe we have to react quickly to an external stimulus, the higher is the density we feel and subsequently our stress level. By creating space, we create the option of *responding* to the requirements of a situation in a level-headed manner instead of merely reacting.

Let's take a look at an example: The next time the phone rings, create space by not immediately taking the call. Maybe you will take the opportunity to consciously take a deep breath before you pick up the phone. Maybe you will create even more space by letting your voicemail pick up and listening to the message before you decide when and how you would like to respond. Besides creating space, this approach benefits good self-management: Reactions triggered by others turn into self-determined actions and you immediately get "ahead of the wave" instead of being inundated by it.

Make it a habit to regularly and consciously create spaces in your daily routine. Initially, these spaces may be small, but they will continue to grow over time. Even a simple break on a hectic day, a chance to go idle and recharge your batteries, creates space. That alone can lead to you being able to better think of and process new ideas and feel less overpowered by an overflowing inbox.

Here are some of the most important ideas that help create external space:
// Learn to say «no».
// Include buffer times in your plans.
// Take conscious breaks.
// Plan uninterrupted work times.
// Go to a quiet environment.
// Forward your calls to someone else or your voicemail.
// Deactivate automatic notifications regarding new text messages or emails.

Creating Internal Space

Internal space is a prerequisite for the previously described self-awareness to have a chance to develop and grow and for you to be able to become an observer of your internal world. As long as we carry a high density of thoughts and a feeling of constriction within us, as long as one thought chases another and we are entangled in our own thinking, as long as our emotions come crashing down on us like waves, we perceive our environment in a similar constrictive and dense way.

If you turn your attention inwards, you can consciously begin to direct your attention towards the space between individual thoughts. Once you start paying attention to it, you will start to consciously notice this space, and that alone will usually lead to relaxation, a reduction of your inner sense of density.

It is possible that this might be difficult for you at first since this approach is different from your perceptual habits. Imagine it like this: You are at a loud concert, at a club or a Techno music event and exposed to a high noise level all night long, the party rocks. Once you have left the event and arrived in the silence of your home, you still hear the buzzing in your ears. Your hearing has been numbed by the loud noise and can't pick up the ticking of your clock or the birds' twitter. This can be compared to the loud thoughts in our head. We are so used to the hum of thoughts that we don't even perceive the fine, subtle and often intuitive internal impulses.

Visualizing the scenario can help in this process: You have probably seen a picture of a hurricane taken from space. Isn't it amazing, this gracefully formed twirl with a dark hole in the middle, the eye of the storm – where everything is still, while all around it, highest wind speeds are raging? Strive to become the eye of the storm in the turmoil of everyday life. No longer get tossed around, get to the core, to the center and attain stillness within your own center. Create a place for yourself to retreat to at any given moment – in the hectic of your day-to-day business, among the flow of hundreds of pedestrians and tourists on Times Square in New York or in the middle of your family life at home. Then, what happens on the outside no longer matters.

The goal is to face any situation you encounter in an appropriate manner, that is responding instead of reacting.

Directing Your Attention

One important key to good self-management lies in regaining control of our attention so that we can direct it like the light beam of a spotlight on the areas in which we need it. Particularly useful in this process are tools which are applied in the training of special forces and pilots. Attention is consciously directed and the restless and chatty rational mind starts to calm down. In a state of attentive presence, we can differentiate between two different kinds of mindfulness or perception: Focus and awareness.

Focus means directing your attention to something in particular – internally or externally. For example, you can focus on a person who is talking to you – despite a lot of noise around you. Just as well, you can focus on internal matters, your breath, a bodily sensation or a certain thought in order to concentrate on thinking about something. Focus is a directed form of attention in a relaxed, yet attentive concentration, like the light beam of a flashlight. In his last book, *"Focus: The Hidden Driver of Excellence"*, Daniel Goleman writes that a good focus can open the door to the flow condition which Mihaly Csikszentmihalyi, the author of the book *"Flow!"*, calls the secret of happiness.

On the other side, there is awareness as a relaxed form of presence. An open form of perception which is not as focused as the light beam of a flashlight, but instead is spread out in all directions, more like the light of a lantern. Both kinds of perception are helpful and useful. And you can alternate between both approaches. Both can be practiced: Just like we train a muscle, our ability to be attentively focused or attentively aware can be increased.

When you focus your attention on something, let's say your breath, then your rational mind will wander and try to take you somewhere else, away from your breath to something else. Here, it is important for you to notice when your mind wanders and drifts away and then gently but firmly bring it back to the object of your focus. Back to your breath, that is, back to your conversation partner or your task.

Focus On The Growing Forest

Over time, you will be able to decide where you would like to direct your attention. Naturally, it will tend to lean towards negative issues. The good news: You can consciously counteract this tendency. This does not imply you should direct your attention away from anything negative and towards the positive, ignoring all negative. This would create a similar distortion of your perception and thus be just as unrealistic. Instead, expand your perception to all of reality. Most of the time, reality consists of positive and negative aspects. Consciously decide where you want your attention and your focus.

Imagine, for example, that the previously mentioned falling tree is a low-performer on your team, a complaining customer, or a colleague who tends to disturb the cooperation within the team. These factors automatically draw our attention to them. Perhaps such an event or behavior even dwarfs everything that goes well. So, in order to notice what is going well, we really have to take a close look. Only then we will recognize the growing forest. Only then we will notice that the little trees have grown a few inches since the last time we checked. But: That is just not as spectacular and does not make as much noise.

Focus On The Here And Now

A Zen monk was asked why he always stayed so calm and collected despite all the things he had going on. He answered:

When I stand, I stand,
When I walk, I walk,
When I sit, I sit,
When I eat, I eat,
When I speak, I speak.

The enquirers interrupted him and said: This is something we do as well, but what is it that you do in addition? He repeated what he had said before. Again, the people said: We do that as well. But he told them:

No, when you sit, you are already standing,
when you stand, you are already walking,
when you walk, you have already reached your destination ...

Observe your rational mind: It tends to either dwell in the past or in the future. Or wander off to any place different from the one you are actually at. Observe yourself when you are waiting somewhere, in line at the supermarket cashier, for example, and notice how the perceived stress increases the more you desire to be somewhere else. In this case, you may want to already be paying for your purchases. When our thoughts dwell in the past, they dwell on memories - based on our negative bias, mainly on negative ones, that is. This lets you experience your past again and again, thus consolidating it and the related stress symptoms. Or your rational mind dwells in the future, either hopefully or − unfortunately more often − picturing something full of concern and drama. Plus, worries come along presenting themselves as incredibly important. The only thing that changes through either thoughts, though, is your overall condition. It gets worse and you react with stress and tension. Instead, just ask yourself: "What kind of problem do I actually have, right at this moment?"

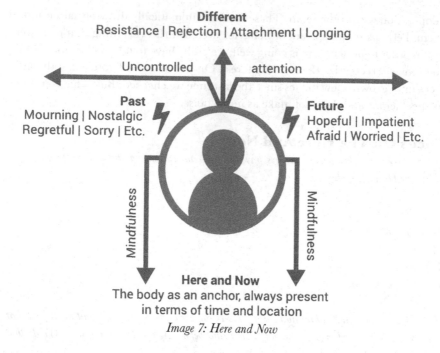

Different
Resistance | Rejection | Attachment | Longing

Uncontrolled attention

Past
Mourning | Nostalgic
Regretful | Sorry | Etc.

Future
Hopeful | Impatient
Afraid | Worried | Etc.

Mindfulness

Mindfulness

Here and Now
The body as an anchor, always present
in terms of time and location

Image 7: Here and Now

In a way, neither the future nor the past exist. They are not real in the moment, they only exist within our thoughts. The only thing that truly exists in reality is always only the now, the current moment. If your rational mind hangs out in the past or future, it is only natural for a certain kind of inner tension to develop. In fact and indeed on a physical level. Whenever you resist the current moment and would rather be somewhere else, or believe you should be somewhere else, inner tension and stress are created. You are not present in the moment.

At the core, it is all a matter of directing your attention, your perception towards the here and now. Mindfulness is nothing more than an awareness exercise in which you consciously pay attention to certain things. Turn waiting in line at the supermarket into an awareness exercise and you will see how the wait will take on a whole new quality.

By taking this approach, your rational mind automatically becomes more quiet. The thought noise becomes less. The loud TV gets turned down and pushed to the background. The goal is to allow the attention to be anchored in the here and now, like a ship out in the ocean drops its anchor to be securely held in position, protected from drifting away even when the sea gets rough. But this kind of fixture is not rigid, it is flexible. Depending on the direction of the wind, the waves and the water current, the ship can turn, but is still anchored to the ground. You can be anchored in the same way and remain in your innermost center, in the calm you carry within you. Your body is a good anchor in this regard.

The body serves as a bridge to the here and now. When you drift away into your internal world with your thoughts and feelings. When you tell yourself stories and allow yourself to get carried away by them, when you subsequently enter into a downward spiral, get worried and increasingly miserable, then you can use your body to redirect your attention to the present moment. By simply paying attention to your breath, for example. The part of your attention which is now directed towards your body, your breath, is no longer available for uncontrolled thinking, can no longer get distracted and drift off course. Instead, it is where it belongs: In the here and now.

Obviously, that does not mean you shouldn't deal with your past. It can be helpful and useful to deal with the past. It allows us to better understand some things, by making ourselves ware of our behavioral patterns, for example. At the same time, though, it does not make sense to define your entire identity through your past or your history. You are no longer the person you were 20 years ago. Then why should you still be telling yourself the same stories about yourself?

Nor does being present in the here and now mean that you shouldn't concern yourself with the future. Of course, you need to plan some things. Of course, it can make sense to think about what the next steps should be. However, you should do that in the here and now, when it is appropriate. And then you can let go of it again. Once you have taken care of the plan for next week, your mind no longer has to be preoccupied with it. It is done.

When you are able to remain in the here and now with your attention, increase the permeability to your internal world while staying calm and relaxed, then you automatically become more open for internal impulses. Then you will still hear the birds twitter even after visiting a loud concert and you are open for intuitive signals which may offer you truly helpful hints.

Focus On Your Circle Of Influence

"Apart from the big tragedies in life which inflict wounds that are slow to heal, we waste lots of precious energy on fighting things that are simply different from what we would like them to be."
JON KABAT-ZINN

Good self-management requires us not to waste too much time and energy on things we cannot influence. It can be helpful to distinguish between the so-called "circle of concern", all the things we think and worry about, and the "circle of influence", all those things we can influence directly, thereby shaping or at least contributing to shaping them.

Steven Covey[17] describes this concept in his book *The Seven Habits of Highly Effective People*. He utilizes the model of "Circles of Influence and Concern" to illustrate the difference between proactive people who have much more control over their emotions and situations and reactive people who are influenced by their emotions and situations in a negative way.

Circles of Influence and Concern (S. Covey)

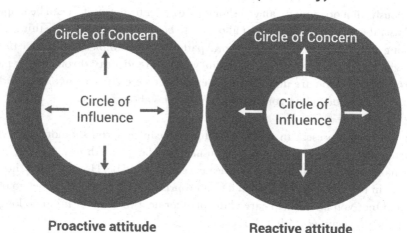

Image 8: "Circles of Concern and Influence" (S. Covey)

The best way to illustrate this phenomenon is – again – the weather: I am sure you know people who get terribly upset about bad weather. They get frustrated and demotivated or even become depressed only because they feel the weather outside is considered "bad". Are we able to control the weather? No. So, why concern yourself with it and spend too much time on resisting it?

In this context, what is your circle of influence? Well, you can choose the right clothes, or be happy about the rain providing much needed water for the plants in your garden. There is no such thing as bad weather, only bad clothing. When you schedule a company event, you can draw up a plan B for inclement weather ahead of time. And who said rain is bad weather anyway?

Often, focusing on your circle of influence even leads to its expansion and you discovering more opportunities to act proactively. Acting in this way sends signals to other people who in turn may meet you with more trust and leeway. On the other hand, people who mainly focus on the circle of concern in which they have no control often feel as though they are victims. They point a finger at others and blame circumstances for their failures. This focusing on negative energy and ignoring the things that can be influenced often leads to the circle of influence being perceived as much smaller than it actually is. So, if you want to be in the driver's seat, focus on the circle of influence – the things you actually can change and control.

Choose Your Attitude

> **"People are not disturbed by things,**
> **but by the view they take of them."**
> EPICTETUS[18]

Even the ancient Greeks knew. There is so much wisdom in this statement, yet we behave differently every single day. We act as though we were the victims of our circumstances or a situation and blame them when we are unhappy.

Recognizing that this simply is not true means taking a big step towards freedom and self-responsibility: It is your very own thinking and evaluating that creates your reality. You are responsible for how you feel and how you are doing. This is one of the most important realizations you can come to in life because it immediately puts you in control of your overall condition. Among the important findings of the last two decade's modern psychology is that as humans, we are able to choose what we think and we can get into the habit of thinking differently (Martin Seligman[19]).

Our automatic, uncontrolled, and continuously evaluating thinking is greatly influenced by our values and convictions. This brings forth thinking habits and patterns. It can truly be said that the uncontrolled, automatic thinking many people exhibit is merely a bad habit which has manifested itself over the course of many years. While it may be ambitious to change the habits of adults and replace them by new ones, it is possible – and starts with an awareness of the current situation. Only then will you be able to consciously choose a different way of thinking.

Picture an employee complaining about something. Maybe he or she is one of those victims who do just that, complain all day long – I am sure you know what kind of person I am talking about. Now it is nine thirty in the morning, you are standing at the coffee maker in your office and you are watching the machine filling your cup. You are enjoying the smell and look forward to drinking your coffee. But then said employee shows up, stops next to you and starts sharing his negative thoughts.

What might be your first inner reaction? Many would think: "Oh no, it's him again! He really gets on my nerves!" Maybe in an even more explicit version. After all, those kinds of spontaneous thoughts and evaluations come along rather clearly. Without being toned down. What kind of feelings do those kinds of thoughts tend to trigger? To what kind of emotional state does that take you? Most likely that would be an emotional cocktail of anger, uncertainty, inferiority, tension, maybe even fear of some form. That in turn leads to a reaction. Usually, this process takes place very quickly and subconsciously.

The key to change lies in being mindful and alert in order to recognize how and what you think and what that does to you. This employee just unloaded all of his trash on you, practically puked it on the floor right in front of your feet and, in a figurative sense, now you get to clean up the mess. He might even feel better afterwards. And you? Once you recognize that it is all a matter of your own thinking, that you do have room to maneuver and influence the course of things, then you can consciously choose to have different thoughts about the situation. Alternative thoughts in such a situation could be: "At least he is still committed, otherwise he would no longer care enough to complain." Or: "This is an opportunity for me to learn and grow." Or you could think: "This poor guy – to see the world in such negative light!", or any other form of unbiased or compassionate thoughts.

When you manage to think like that, what kind of emotions will that likely trigger? Quite different ones, obviously: Self-confidence, relaxation, calmness, curiosity... A different emotional cocktail, one that has a much more positive impact on you and your overall condition. So, the key is to consciously replace the often negative, automatic thoughts with more realistic, constructive or even positive ones.

A prerequisite for that is improving how well you listen to yourself. Dealing with your thoughts, emotions and ultimately stress, primarily is a listening exercise. The better you perceive your inner voice – your thoughts and emotions – the better you recognize your needs. The more likely you are to align your behavior and your communication with them. The best moment to handle negative emotions is the moment you start to sense them. It is much more difficult to interrupt an emotional pattern once it is fully established. However, this requires that inner permeability, access to your internal world – your inner thinking and feeling. Or, to put it simply: You have to be in touch with yourself.

You Are What You Think

If you have ever seen a ski race on TV, you are familiar with the close-ups of the athletes. Shortly before the start of the race you can observe them in the racer's tuck position, mentally going down the slope, with their eyes closed. But what they do is not limited to that. They do something that is pivotal: They visualize victory – knowing the difference this makes for their performance. Or do you think any ski racer would vividly picture himself losing the race right before it starts? Can you believe that this does indeed make a huge difference?

This is true not only for ski races, but for everything. Particularly in business, where presenting in front of others is one of the biggest fears people have. Generally, presenting is at the top of the list of the greatest fears, next to fear of heights, fear of enclosed spaces or fear of spiders. Or, like Mark Twain[20] put it: "The brain is an organ that starts to work as soon as you are born and doesn't stop until you get up to deliver a speech."

For many people, there is something threatening about this, which is why it gets so much attention. Our attention is automatically directed at anything that is considered a threat or potentially negative. However, you still have a choice: Are you alert and mindful enough to realize how worried you are, how you dive into your fears, only intensifying them? Do you notice how your fear of failure transforms into images, how you picture yourself standing in front of the audience, failing miserably? And: Do you notice how those images affect your emotional and physical condition?

Let's try this experiment: Slowly and as consciously as possible, read the following lines and vividly imagine ...

- // How you are standing in your kitchen
- // You open the refrigerator and discover a plate with three lemons
- // You reach for the plate, take it out and put it on the desk
- // You grab a knife and a cutting board and put both next to the plate
- // Now you take one of the lemons and put it on the cutting board
- // You cut it in half and then again in two halves, so that you end up with a quarter lemon in your hand
- // Then you picture yourself bringing this fresh, juicy-sour smelling lemon to your face – smelling it once again and then savoring a hearty bite ...

// ... sucking up the sour lemon juice, letting it flow back and forth in your mouth, thoroughly enjoying the acid taking hold of your entire palate, your throat and finally pleasurably swallowing it

So, did you feel something? Maybe how your salivary glands started to produce saliva. How the muscles in your mouth contracted and became a bit tense? Maybe how you make a grimace due to the sour taste? In this experiment, most people experience one or several of the described physical sensations.

What does that mean? At that moment, your brain is incapable of distinguishing between a real lemon and an imaginary lemon. In fact, your entire body reacts to the imaginary lemon when you picture yourself biting into it. Savor that fact, for a moment: What you think and imagine all day long directly impacts your emotional and physical condition. Your body reacts with the classical stress symptoms to any negative thoughts, fears, worries, concerns and horror scenarios that you picture.

The typical stress reaction of the body to potential danger means that it provides maximum energy and performance capability for two different strategies in dealing with danger: Fight or flight. Both strategies require this maximum performance capability and the body provides it by doing various things:

// It releases adrenaline
// If the stress continues, it secretes cortisol
// Blood supply is increased to ensure an adequate oxygen supply of the organs
// The pulse rises
// Transpiration increases in order to cool down the body in this phase of maximum performance

The list could be continued. It makes no difference whether there is an acute threat or you only imagine it. Especially when the physical reactions take place over a prolonged period of time, e.g. when you have to work in a climate shaped by fear and distrust, they naturally take a sustainably negative toll on your health.

If you manage to notice all of this with an observant attitude, you can decide to paint a different picture instead and think other thoughts: By envisioning how the people you address will approach you afterwards to thank you for your great speech. How your boss will pad you on the back after the meeting and tell you: "Thank you! That was an excellent presentation!" If you envision that kind of success as frequently and as vividly as possible, this will have an effect as well – one that can be physically measured.

In short: We should be mindful about what we think because it has a much greater impact than most of us are aware of – particularly on our health, our happiness and even the way we feel in general.

The Valley Of Tears

Similarly, the way we handle our emotions has a physical effect. You may know the feeling when you are upset and get all tense, or when anger leads to the heat rising in your head and your pulse beginning to race. A lot of people experience these kinds of emotions as "negative" due to the unpleasant feeling they involve and handle them in an unhealthy way by exploding – causing collateral damage regarding relationships – or imploding, that is, hiding their feelings. Either approach is unhealthy in the long-run. At the same time, it would be an illusion to believe that life could be lived without any challenging emotions. Emotions are our primary evaluation system, so they have a decisive and often self-protective function. The determining factor is how we deal with them – with our own emotions and with those of others. It can be challenging not to react with anger to someone else's anger. Particularly for executives, but also for those working in direct customer contact, emotional control is vitally important.

What happens when we show a strong emotional reaction, let's say due to a surprising and unpleasant change we experience? We enter into a process that resembles a curve with a deep valley, we will call it "the valley of tears". Like many similar concepts, this model is rooted in the grief cycle described by Elisabeth Kübler-Ross[21], a pioneer in thanatology.

Let me use a specific example to walk you through the valley of tears and let's take a look at the stages you typically go through in such a situation: Imagine you have booked a flight for your vacation. You pack your luggage and drive to the airport. There you check the big departure board to find out which gate your flight departs from. You find your flight, but next to it you discover big red letters spelling the word "Cancelled"!

Phase 1: Denial / Resistance
"Oh no, this can't be true!" is the most likely internal – and possibly external – reaction to that information. You are in the first stage, the stage of denial and refuse to believe what is taking place.

Phase 2: Anger / Resentment

Inner rejection and resistance towards the situation often lead to anger or resentment, which can express itself in various ways, depending on your personality. Picture yourself starting to get upset about the cancellation of your flight: "What in the world? How dare they!?" – and you can feel the anger rising in you.

Phase 3: Sadness / Disconcertion

Anger and resentment often give way to the next phase, a phase of disconcertion which usually expresses itself in a mix of sadness and worries: "What if I can't get on another flight today? What if I can't find another flight at all to get to my destination?!"

Phase 4: Rationalization

It isn't until you have made it through these first phases that you reach the bottom of the curve, the valley of tears, rock bottom. It is the point at which rational thinking slowly but surely becomes possible again. You can start making sense of the situation and think: "What are my options? What can I do?" Slowly, the resistance dissolves and you can turn towards the future and potential solutions.

Phase 5: Decision

Once you have determined your options, you need to make a decision. Will you go straight back home, or contact the next airline counter? Or will you go have a beer first?

Phase 6: Acceptance and Reorientation

Now that you have decided what needs to be done you can finally accept the situation for what it is and direct all of your attention towards resolving it.

Phase 7: Engagement / Commitment

In the final phase you wholeheartedly say «yes» to the change, you completely let go and invest your energy in the new situation. You have successfully walked through the valley of tears and left it behind.

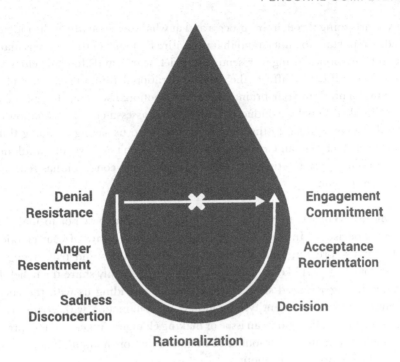

**Denial
Resistance**

**Engagement
Commitment**

**Anger
Resentment**

**Acceptance
Reorientation**

**Sadness
Disconcertion**

Decision

Rationalization

The image shows one variant of the well-known "Change Curve". Its origin is based on the results of the sociological thanatology research conducted by Elisabeth Kübler-Ross. Subsequently, the model has been adopted by various other authors and transferred to a business context.

Image 9: Valley of Tears

It is important to realize that this is a natural process which we enter whenever we are confronted with what we believe to be negative changes. Depending on the severity and personal attitude, this process can take quite a while to complete. Losing a loved one obviously means dealing with grief on a much greater scale and involves a longer grief process than being at the airport and finding out that your flight has been cancelled.

Generally, there is no shortcut from the first phase to the last: There is no way around or over it, but only right through it. Therefore, to me, the expression of "getting over" something is misleading. I prefer the expression of "getting through" something. The way out is through.

It is not very helpful to try to ignore the negative emotions which occur at the beginning of the curve and not to be willing to admit to yourself that you are angry, said, upset or scared: It is key to walk through this process in the best careful, attentive and effective way. It does help for you to recognize for yourself that you are going through this process and at what stage you are at the moment. It is also important to understand that the entire first part of this curve is mainly shaped by emotions – anger, resentment, grief, fear – and that this emotional condition significantly affects the clear and rational thinking abilities of the "executive center" in your brain: The more emotional we are, the less we are able to think rationally, conduct a level-headed assessment of a situation and make decisions. Amongst other things, this leads to us saying or doing things under the influence of an emotional fog which we don't even realize until much later, or even regret in retrospect, when our emotional condition has reached a normal level again.

This means: When the emotions are raging high, it is best not to make any important decisions. Instead, be attentive and become aware of your emotions, maybe even express it, talk about it, name the emotions and truly recognize and accept them. Just like my colleague John Parr, I firmly share the belief that particularly anger indeed serves the purpose of providing us with the energy we require to focus on identifying solutions, in conjunction with giving us the motivation to actually resolve an issue or making changes. Anger that is expressed in an authentic manner, without attacking, blaming or manipulating someone, thus is a highly productive emotion.

With this approach, you will be much quicker to reach the point of the curve at which the waves of emotions have calmed down and clear thinking is possible again. So, allow yourself to enter and get through this entire curve, consciously live through your emotions - and take all the time you need for this process.

Be Your Own Friend

If you have ever been a passenger on a plane, you are familiar with the safety instructions. Part of these instructions is the explanation of the use of the oxygen masks which fall from the cabin ceiling in case of a sudden loss in cabin pressure. The usual cruising altitude of modern aircrafts is around flight level 350 and higher, which equals around 10,000 meters or 35,000 feet or more. At this altitude, the so-called "time of useful consciousness" (TUC) is very short: The air pressure is so low that the oxygen concentration in the breathable air is no longer sufficient to provide the level of oxygen the brain needs. This means: In case of decompression, that is, a sudden loss of pressure, you lose consciousness within a matter of thirty to sixty seconds. For this reason, the air pressure in the cabin of an aircraft is increased to one that equals an altitude of 1,600 to 2,500 meters or 5,200 to 8,200 feet. In other words, the air pressure you feel when you are at the top of a mountain which is about 2,000 meters or 6,000 feet high, is similar to the one you feel on an airplane.

During the safety instructions provided by the crew, you will be told: "If there is a sudden loss of cabin pressure, first, pull your oxygen mask over your face, continue to breathe normally and only then assist other passengers." When we assume that the time we have to react only lasts thirty to sixty seconds, it is only logical that first you must ensure your own oxygen supply before you can help others. What good would it do your child or fellow passengers if you were about to help them with putting on their mask and lose consciousness in the process?

These instructions can easily be transferred to other areas in life – and to the essence of this book: First, you must ensure that you are well in touch with yourself, stable, in your center and in a state of good balance, before you can truly provide for others. I am sure you know the principle "Love your neighbor as you love yourself." The way I see it, the second part of this sentence is the one that is more important – and the one which unfortunately often gets neglected. This doesn't have anything to do with selfishness or egocentricity, but only with the fact that you will not be able to give someone your full attention and support while you yourself are unstable, stressed, or full of self-doubt.

Once you begin to recognize your worth and give yourself the level of appreciation you have always expected and hoped to receive from others, but maybe never received the way you had hoped for, your personal freedom sets in. Then you no longer place so much value on whether or not you receive recognition and appreciation from an external source because you are so well connected with yourself and in such an amicable relationship shaped by so much appreciation that you no longer depend on receiving any kind of recognition and appreciation from an external source.

I've spent too many years at war with myself
The doctor has told me it's no good for my health
STING
(CONSIDER ME GONE)

Have you ever asked yourself how friendly you act towards yourself? Maybe you are among those people who are more critical with themselves than they would ever be with their best friend. Then you are in good company. When you gain greater proximity to yourself, ideally you will reach a point at which you will be able to develop a favorable, an amicable relationship with yourself.

Make a conscious decision to become a good friend of yours. This has something to do with forgiving: Where do you still blame yourself for things that happened a long time ago? Where would you have forgiven a good friend a long time ago, but still judge yourself harshly? What would happen if you were to realize that back then, you did the best you could at the time. And what would it feel like if, based on that, you were to simply let go?

Start treating yourself like you would treat a good friend. This will change your entire relationship with yourself, your inner dialogues and it will obviously have a far-reaching impact on how you treat yourself - and subsequently how you treat others.

///

STOPOVER - I

Use your own words to summarize what you have learned for yourself in this last chapter and what kind of information you consider to be the most important or helpful for you.

_____

_____

_____

_____

_____

_____

_____

_____

_____

Think about the findings you would like to transfer to your professional or personal life. What kind of intentions have already begun to take root and where do you see opportunities to put them into practice?

_____

_____

_____

_____

_____

_____

_____

_____

///

INTERPERSONAL COMPETENCE
///

Based on the three main aspects of personal competence, interpersonal competence encompasses three main areas as well:

1. Situational and Social Awareness
Are you aware of what is going on around you at all times? Are you in control of the situation? This can be crucial, e.g. in a conflict talk. Are you aware of your position in the structure of a conversation and do you realize what is happening on the relationship level? Or are you completely absorbed in the content of the conversation and running on autopilot? Can you detect emotions in other people and recognize the early signs of conflict in time?

2. Communication
When it comes to entering into authentic contact with others and reaching common goals together, then communication is the key. With all its facets, communication is the link that connects us, which we can use to synchronize and harmonize with each other. Are you able to communicate in a careful and appreciative manner and assume responsibility for your share regarding the quality of the communication?

3. Relationship Management
If we want to make contact, establish a relationship and maintain it even under difficult circumstances, we need to apply conscious relationship management. Relationships are like plants – they die when we don't take care of them. In cases of conflict, do you have the ability to de-escalate and behave in a way that preserves the relationship and still resolve the conflict? So that in the end, a satisfactory result is reached for all parties involved and everyone can part in "okay"-mode?

Image 10: Interpersonal Competence

SITUATIONAL AND SOCIAL AWARENESS
//

We were in Hong Kong and ready for our return flight, just waiting for our passengers to board. Our schedule had taken us on a Boeing 747 from Zurich to the Indian harbor city of Mumbai. A few days later, we had flown from there to Hong Kong, where, after a spectacular approach, we landed at the old airport of Kai Tak. At that time, the approach procedure involved practically flying towards the final approach in a right angle and required the cockpit crew to make a sharp right turn low above the roofs of Hong Kong right before touchdown. Particularly on the old lady, the B747, this was always a special experience.

But now we were ready for our return flight from Hong Kong to Mumbai. The first passengers arrived at the door and I greeted them with a smile. After a while, a frowning elderly lady walked up. She did not greet or even look at me. I directed her to the other aisle and asked my younger colleague to take her to her seat in business class.

A while later, that colleague came back to me and complained about the unfriendliness of the lady. She said she hoped that passenger wouldn't ruin the whole flight for us, with her sour attitude and unfriendliness. I replied that it was up to us and only up to us to decide whether we would allow someone to ruin our mood or not.

We finished all necessary preparations for the flight and took off for India. Once we had reached our cruising altitude, I went on my round through first and business class to personally welcome our passengers and introduce myself. I did so with the elderly lady in seat 10 J as well, when I noticed she had tears in her eyes. There wasn't anyone in the seat next to her and I asked if she would allow me to take a seat for a moment. She nodded and so I sat down. "Is there anything I can do for you?", I asked. She looked at me and shook her head. "I just lost my husband.", she said. "He died a few days ago while we were in Hong Kong. Now I am taking him home."

All at once I was able to understand her behavior towards us and obviously saw it in a completely different light. She had lost her husband and his corpse was below us in the cargo compartment of our aircraft. I informed the crew accordingly. For the rest of the flight, there was a special bond that had been created between the lady and me. All of a sudden, there was something almost loving in her facial expression and she became friendlier even towards the other members of the crew, although I chose to personally take care of her for the rest of the flight.

This example illustrates the filters of perception we are equipped with, filters made up of our values, convictions and belief systems and all of our previous experiences. It also shows how quickly we assess, evaluate and often even judge what we perceive through our filters. In the meantime, an entirely different reality takes place right in front of our eyes – which we don't see due to our evaluation of the situation. Life consists of many repetitions. Thus, there is a risk of us going into autopilot by falling back into our preconceived notions and automatically doing and evaluating a lot of things instead of being present and attentive in the current moment.

Imagine you have an encounter with a new colleague, customer, or employee. Maybe something about the person bothers or upsets you and manifests itself in your first impression of him or her. A while later, you go to a meeting – and who do you find sitting at the table? That person! Now, if you are not very careful and attentive in that moment, the filter of your first impression will cloud your view of the person and the situation. In the worst case, you will no longer see the human being sitting in front of you, but only the image you have of him or her. Even worse: You adjust your behavior to this concept of yours. However, maybe the person only had a bad day when you first met, or you had a bad day – which may have distorted your perception.

We are all subject to this natural, human behavior. But we can do something to stop this process. It takes two things to enable us to reduce – or even eliminate – the influence of our filters and our tendency to evaluate everything:

1. Make yourself aware of your filters
Keep reminding yourself of the fact that your experiences of the past can have a negative impact on your present and may even hinder you. Recognize that fixed, preconceived notions and concepts may obstruct your view of what really matters. With this realization alone, you will win half the battle.

2. Reset your filters on a regular basis
Be attentive as often as you can and pay close attention to whether you might be entering into a situation or an encounter with a preconceived notion or fixed opinion. If the answer is "yes", push the "reset" button in your head by consciously setting aside any preconceived notion and instead, try to take a fresh, unbiased look at the situation. The often quoted "beginner's mind" provides you with the perfect attitude. It means you give yourself, the situation, and all people involved a new chance. Any setting in which relationships play a role, particularly in leadership, sales, and customer service and in any kind of cooperation and co-existence, this simple principle serves to significantly and sustainably improve the quality of those relationships.

Situational Awareness
Situational awareness describes a state in which you are alert and attentive towards your environment. Good situational awareness is particularly important in any setting in which technological and situational complexity pose a challenge for the people involved. It is a demanding, yet indispensable prerequisite for many complex work environments such as aviation, air traffic control, maritime navigation, surgical teams in health environments, emergency organizations and military operations, or the operational management of oil drilling platforms and nuclear plants.

This means situational awareness is also an essential aspect of the work of cabin crew on board an airplane. Especially during take-off and landing, all senses are directed towards detecting any kind of change and deviation of the norm. This applies to issues of a visual, acoustic and olfactory nature, such as smells. Ideally, even during cruise flight, part of the crew's attention always lies on the various aspects of the overall situation. This includes cabin temperature, the overall mood of the passengers, particularly special or noticeably different behavior of individuals, the condition of colleagues and unusual smells and noises.

Being 100% aware of the situation during the flight is of utmost importance for the cockpit crew as well – because it is safety relevant. The term "situational awareness" is used in aviation and describes the conscious and at all times alert assessment of the current situation and potential changes as well as their influence. Pilots of a modern passenger jet continuously check the cockpit instruments which display the condition of the aircraft, its position (flight phase and course) and its external environment (weather conditions). When flying a smaller sports plane, situational awareness is characterized to a greater extent by a direct perception of the various aspects while on a commercial aircraft, it involves monitoring many complex and automated systems. Another additional aspect is cooperating with a whole team.

Generally, anyone will benefit from pursuing the ability to display a 360-degree awareness. Plus, the good news is that it can be trained in a relaxed, yet sustainable way.

More Of An Attitude Than A Technique

It is important to understand that situational awareness is rather an attitude than a technique. This is why it is a skill which can be exercised not only by personnel who have been trained and educated accordingly, but in fact by anyone who comes up with the desire and necessary discipline it requires.

The most essential element in the process is recognizing that – depending on the environment you are in - irregularities, problems, challenges and, in the worst case, threatening circumstances do in fact exist. Ignoring or negating them significantly reduces the likelihood of recognizing them as soon as possible. In all aspects of life – and particularly in business life – achievements and welcome events go hand in hand with challenges and problems. Once one issue has been solved, it is very likely to be succeeded by the next one. Recognizing and accepting that alone already makes dealing with it easier. Being in denial of those facts would be nothing but naïve and, in the worst case, apathy or self-complacency could be fatal.

Another element of highly-developed situational awareness involves learning to trust your gut feeling, your intuition. Here, self- and situational awareness are directly interlinked, which means they actually cannot be separated. Just like a part of your attention should always be like the light of a lantern, shining around you 360 degrees, another part should always remain within your inner core, being attentive to internal signals and clues. Often, we subconsciously perceive signs of danger or potential problems we can barely notice nor describe with the use of our rational mind. How often have you told yourself or others: "I saw that coming!" or "I knew this would happen!". There are enough reports of people who did perceive the early signs of troubles or dangers and chose to ignore them – and suffered the consequences. Trusting your intuition and your emotions may feel uncomfortable, but ignoring them can lead to serious problems.

Levels Of Situational Awareness

Most people are familiar with the various sleep phases. To put it simply, you can differentiate between light sleep, the so-called rapid-eye-movement – or REM for short – phase, and dreamless deep sleep. During the night, these phases alternate. This means we move from a phase of light sleep in which we also dream to deep sleep in which our physical and mental activities are reduced to a minimum.

Comparable conditions exist during wakefulness: We normally find ourselves at one of four levels of situational awareness. There are many ways to describe these four stages. The easiest one is to compare the stages with the level of attention we display when driving a car, something every driver knows from experience. For convenience purposes, let's call them "inattentive", "relaxed-aware", "focused-attentive" and "alarmed".

The first level, inattentive, can be compared to driving along a well-familiar road, or driving while absorbed in thought, a daydream or a song we listen to on the radio, or the screaming children in the backseat. Omnipresent smartphones also have an increasing tendency to cause inattentiveness among drivers. Have you ever driven somewhere, thinking about an important issue on the way and arriving at your destination without remembering how you got there? If your answer is "yes", then you were operating on the level of "inattentive" at the time.

The second level, "relaxed-aware", is considered to be the desirable condition. It corresponds to defensive driving. It is a condition in which you are relaxed, but still keeping an eye on other vehicles, watching traffic in front of you in an anticipatory manner, proactively scanning your environment for potential dangers. If, for example, you approach a cross-walk and you notice a group of children playing on the side of the road, you prepare yourself for possibly having to hit the brakes, should one of the children run into the street. Defensive driving with a relaxed-aware attentiveness is not particularly tiring and can be maintained for an extended period of time, if you muster up the discipline not to drift away into inattentiveness. When driving in this condition, you can still enjoy the drive, look at the landscape and listen to the radio, without allowing yourself to be distracted by something to the extent of everything else being shut out. You can consciously take on this attitude during a conversation, a meeting or while fulfilling a different professional or personal task.

The next stage of situational awareness, "focused-attentive", resembles a drive during difficult road conditions, such as icy or slushy roads or a road riddled with potholes and full of adventurous drivers, like I have seen in many countries. Driving under such conditions means keeping both hands on the steering wheel and all of your attention on the road in front of you and the traffic around you. Answering a phone call is out of the question, so is allowing yourself to get distracted by anything else. The level of concentration this requires is demanding and tiring and can turn an otherwise easy drive into an exhausting and stressful experience because it requires sustained and absolute focus.

The fourth and final stage is "alarmed". This condition usually comes with an adrenaline rush. It happens when one of the children who were just playing on the side of the road runs out into the street right in front of your car. The stage of alarmed can be frightening, but you are still able to fully function at this stage. You can perform an emergency stop and still control your vehicle. The adrenaline rush can even support you in reacting quickly and with the necessary power as well as determination.

Beyond the fourth stage, there is only shock, a condition in which we are petrified and unable to react. This can even feel as if you are no longer part of the situation, but merely an observer of what is happening. Often, this experience comes with a sense of time slowing down significantly. Research has shown that this condition is often induced in passengers of an airplane who experience an emergency in which they see no way to escape. The passengers will not move until the escape route is pointed out to them, for example by a flight attendant during the evacuation of the airplane.

The Right Level At The Right Time

Now that we have taken a closer look at the various levels of situational awareness, we want to identify and consciously take on the appropriate attitude in any given moment. Our body and our mind need to be able to relax, so it is obviously important for us to get enough sleep. When we are sitting at home, in front of the TV or reading a book, it certainly is quite alright to be in "inattentive" mode. Unfortunately, though, there are some people who are at that level even when it is absolutely inappropriate, like at night in a poorly lit neighborhood in an unfamiliar city. If we are inattentive while we are driving and a child runs into the street or a car in front of us unexpectedly hits the brakes, we don't see the problem coming. This means we either overlook the danger which makes it impossible for us to avoid it or we freeze and do not react at all. Neither option is a good one. These things happen because it is very difficult to change the level of situational awareness in an expedited way. This is particularly true when there are several levels which have to be passed, as would be the case from "inattentive" to "alarmed". That would be like putting the transmission directly from the first gear into the sixth.

A high level of situational awareness does not mean being paranoid, overanxious or obsessively attentive. In fact, it is quite challenging to maintain a condition of focused attentiveness over an extended period of time, and state of alarm can only be maintained for a short period before leading to exhaustion. The natural fight or flight reflex can be very helpful when it is controlled and subsequently lifted accordingly. When that is not the case and our system is exposed to a continuously high level of adrenaline, cortisol and other endogenous substances which are released upon feelings of stress, then, over time, that is unhealthy and can lead to stress-related symptoms.

So, it is not about being at the highest level of alarmed or focused attention. We are, quite simply, not made for that. Even the best-trained specialist needs time for rest and recuperation. For this reason, relaxed awareness is the desirable condition that can be maintained for an extended period of time, without the effort the two higher levels require. Relaxed awareness is not tiring and allows us to enjoy life while we are still able to react to events – when necessary. Whenever we move in the outside world and are therefore subject to sudden unexpected events – which is practically always the case – we should spend most of that time in the mode of relaxed awareness.

Then, if we notice something unusual which has the potential of becoming challenging or even threatening, we can shift into a higher gear, into focused-attentive, and continue to observe the situation. If we were wrong, we can go ahead and shift our awareness back down again. On the other hand, should the situation in fact turn into a potential threat, our anticipation can help tremendously in averting an escalation. In that case, it may not even be necessary to move to the level of "alarmed" thanks to the fact that we were able to recognize the problem early on and act accordingly.

Examples of this can be found in wildlife as well. During several stays in East Africa, I had the opportunity to watch the local animals on several safaris. Gnus and zebras, for instance, live in a symbiotic relationship. Gnus benefit from the constantly high level of alertness zebras display. The change from relaxed awareness while grazing to focused-attentive, with their head held high and their eyes wide open, up to alarmed when danger is close can be well observed. Zebras on the other hand benefit from the gnus because should they have to kick into flight mode, gnus are much slower and thus more likely to fall victim to a predator than a zebra.

This flexibility regarding your level of situational awareness can be trained with the help of simple exercises you can integrate into daily life. For instance, over the course of the day, you can occasionally consciously raise your situational awareness to the level of focused-attentive for a short period of time. After checking into a hotel and getting to your room, for example, you can study the escape and rescue plan you find on your door and familiarize yourself with the closest emergency exit. Or, after finding your seat on an airplane, you identify the closest emergency exit there and count the number of seat rows between you and the exit. Actually, the closest emergency exit is not necessarily the door through which you entered.

Social Awareness

Just like self-awareness, social awareness is about the conscious perception of emotional conditions, feelings and needs. In this case, it doesn't just focus on your own, but on those of other people. A different term for that is »social sensitivity«.

One important element of social sensitivity is empathy: The ability and willingness to take on the emotions, feelings, views and standpoints of other people, and understand and comprehend them, which means being able and willing to put yourself in someone else's position.

In the environment of organizations and businesses, social sensitivity also encompasses the ability to recognize the dynamics, relationships and needs of an entire group and consider them adequately. In customer interaction, this is primarily a matter of service orientation. It involves anticipating customer needs, identifying them and being able to meet them accordingly. As with self-awareness, it is in effect a question of recognizing the dynamics and emotions and handling them appropriately.

Social sensitivity is an essential part of emotional intelligence. It leads to greater trust, group identity, network and relationship building and subsequently to more contributions, commitment and cooperation. Ultimately, it paves the way to making better decisions, finding more creative solutions and simply being more productive.

Particularly in leadership, but also in working with others and in customer contact, a major role is played by recognizing the existing needs and, ideally, meeting them. With empathy as your foundation for social awareness, it is easier to say or do the right thing in any given situation, reduce fear and the effects of anger, limit damage, or unite and strengthen the positive emotional drivers of a team.

Early Detection Is Key

In the context of averting and de-escalating conflicts, it is crucial to recognize the signs of conflict early on and address them decisively so that an escalation of the conflict can be avoided. Social sensitivity and communication play major parts in this process. But what are the early signs we need to look for? First and foremost, there is a decline in the quality of communication. Often, it becomes insincere with sarcastic and ironic remarks finding their way into the conversation. Sarcasm is a form of aggression disguised as humor. The tone gets louder, unfriendlier, more aggressive – the perceived quality of the "we" changes, which can be expressed in a verbal (words), paraverbal (tone) or nonverbal (body language) way. On the verbal level, a significant increase in the use of the word "but" can be an indicator for the rising conflict potential.

At the same time, nonverbal expression quickly reveals potential irritation or disturbances on the relationship level. I want to emphasize, though, that these are not necessarily indicators that are true for any kind of nonverbal expression. For instance, if someone sits in a meeting with his or her arms crossed and leaning back right from the start, that does not necessarily mean that this person is resisting or withdrawn and unwilling to open up. It may simply be a comfortable position for him or her.

If, however, the nonverbal expression of a participant changes significantly over the course of a meeting, then that can be an indicator for a potential disruption on the relationship level. An example for that kind of situation could be that someone was leaning forward and maintaining eye contact for quite a while, showing an open posture and actively taking part in the discussion - and then, at some point, leans back, folds his arms, crosses his legs and looks away.

Distorted perception is another indicator for conflict: If even the slightest remark is interpreted very negatively, you can assume that the other person is becoming more sensitive and his or her perception might be distorted. Obviously, conflict potential also increases when a basic attitude is shaped by distrust rather than trust and manifested through the corresponding behavior.

This principle applies: Sharpen your perception and, ideally, refrain from interpreting, evaluating and judging.

COMMUNICATION

///

When it comes to effective interaction with other people, communication is obviously the most important tool. It is the link building a bridge between "I" and "you", and it has the power to turn the two into a "we".

But what exactly is interpersonal communication? It is not only about exchanging information – as is the case when two technical devices communicate. Primarily, it is about making contact on the relationship level while establishing and preserving relationships. And herein lies the problem of the societal change over the last decades: The ability to exchange information and data has increased exponentially. In times in which relationships are ended via WhatsApp and jobs terminated via SMS, it becomes obvious how big the distance between people has grown and how small the willingness has become to enter into true contact. What suffers in this process is authentic interpersonal dialogue. The dialogue in the form of an intense exchange between two people, defined by more than just exchanging information.

Still, as a synonym for communication between people, I like using a term from the technical environment: Synchronization. What do you do when you synchronize two technical devices, for example a smartphone and a laptop (assuming it works)? You reach a form of equalization. Following the synchronization, both devices have the same data. This can be transferred to communication between people: If communication is successful, all parties share the same understanding of what was discussed.

Why does it make sense to think about communication at all? We start to communicate almost as soon as we are born – actually, even before. It only takes one, maybe two years before we start to talk, use words to communicate with others. And then we continue to do so throughout our lives. So why should we invest any more time and energy on the topic – if it is one of the most natural things in the world?

This is one way of looking at it. At the same time, though, it is safe to say that there is nothing more persistent than the illusion that you only have to open your mouth in order to be understood. Every day – in business, in our personal life, practically anywhere – we can see that this is not the case.

"What is thought is not yet said,
What is said is not properly heard,

What is heard is not properly understood,
What is understood is not always accepted,
What is accepted is not always applied,
What is applied is not always kept."[22]

More often than we are aware of, we react to what we hear – which is not necessarily what was said. One of the biggest and most common misconceptions in communication is actually the assumption that it took place. There are some basic principles of communication you should know. They form an essential foundation for behaving in a way that promotes communication and preserves relationships.

The first and most important principle of interpersonal communication was defined by Paul Watzlawick, one of the best-known communication scientists and sociologists: "One cannot not communicate." As soon as you are in contact with another person, you communicate. That does not necessarily mean that you utter words, because even when you do not speak, you still communicate. Maybe even more so than if you were to say something. For: "If someone no longer talks to you, he wants to tell you something by doing so."[23]

That means you communicate on different levels and the spoken word is only one of three levels that contribute to the overall communication – and the overall effect you have on others:

// Verbal communication – the spoken word
// Paraverbal communication – the tone in which something is said
// Nonverbal communication – gestures, facial expression, body posture

A second important principle of communication is that communication is always as well, meaning body language plays a significant role. When I ask people where they think nonverbal communication may not be part of communication, I often get the answer: "On the phone, there is no nonverbal aspect." This is only partially true. Communication is not perceived visually, but it still takes place and has an effect on the third dimension of the overall effect, the paraverbal aspect. The French say: "C'est le ton qui fait la musique" – It is the tone which makes the music. The same applies to communication. The way you say something – and I am sure you know this from personal experience – can make a big difference. Only in written communication, the nonverbal part is entirely missing – which is one of the reasons why there are now hundreds of emoticons we can use to try to avoid potential misunderstandings.

In the overall impact – especially when there is a discrepancy between what you are saying, how you are saying it and your nonverbal expression – the nonverbal expression always wins. Albert Mehrabian[24] developed the so-called 7-38-55-rule which describes the relation between the impact of verbal, paraverbal and nonverbal expression when these aspects are contradictory. According to Mehrabian, the impact is determined through spoken content (verbal) by only 7 percent, by 38 percent through the tone (paraverbal) and by 55 percent – more than half – by the body language (nonverbal). That means: Consciously pay attention to your own, nonverbal expression and sharpen your perception for the nonverbal signals of others.

The Power Of Words

In 2011, the promotion video «The Power of Words» published by the Scottish agency Purplefeather went viral on YouTube and created a global sensation. It shows in an impressive way how a conscious choice of words can indeed change our world. A blind man is sitting on the ground in a pedestrian zone and asking for donations. There is a small tin can in front of him in which passersby are supposed to throw the change they carry. Next to him, there is a cardboard sign that says: "I'm blind, please help." However, this business model does not seem to be working too well. Only occasionally, a coin makes it into the tin can, nothing more.

After a while, a young woman walks up. She stops and takes a quick look at the sign, picks it up, writes something on the back and puts it back so that her writing is visible to the people walking by. Without saying a word, she continues walking. Business seems to pick up immediately as soon as she is gone: More and more passersby are putting their change into the can. When the camera pans out to the cardboard sign, her words can finally be read: "It's a beautiful day. And I can't see it."

Where is the difference between these two statements that causes such a different reaction by the people walking by? Apparently, the first statement – I am blind, please help – is a rather rational one. Most people waking by probably think something along the lines of "Is that even true?" or "Leave me alone, I've got enough issues of my own" which leads to only an occasional coin ending up in the tin can.

The second statement – It's a beautiful day. And I can't see it. – has a completely different effect, that is, an emotional one: The first part makes us realize that it is indeed a beautiful day and it ignites a feeling of gratitude and connectedness in us. The second part - ... and I can't see it – primarily triggers empathy and compassion. This makes for a powerful combination leading to the desired action.

The Canadian neurologist Donald Calne brings the effect to the point: "The essential difference between emotion and reason is that emotion leads to action while reason leads to conclusions." The neuroscientist Antonio Damasio explains in his book *Descartes' Error: Emotion, Reason and the Human Brain*: "We are not thinking machines that feel. We are feeling machines that think."

Now if such a small cause can have such a great effect, what does that mean for our daily interactions? Do we want conclusions or do we want action? And how often do we say things which are clear from an objective perspective, but, on an emotional level, fail to have the desired effect or worse, have an opposite effect?

Irritating Expressions And Relationship-Preserving Alternatives

In communication, a conscious choice of words is paramount because words trigger associations in your counterpart. This happens within a matter of seconds: You hear or read a term and your brain literally starts to "google". It develops associations which in turn cause positive or negative emotions which have a direct impact on your internal and external reaction as well as your decision-making.

This means that by your choice of words, you can significantly contribute to the level of quality of communication. But, hand on heart: How consciously do you choose your words in the pursuit of contributing to the quality of communication through positive associations? And, on the other side, how often do you unconsciously choose words which are not conducive because they trigger negative emotional reactions and strain the relationship? Such expressions are called "irritating". Often, they may be okay on a factual level. On the relationship level, though, they are problematic and can lead to irritation and disruption.

But ...

One of the most important irritating expressions is the word "but". An inconspicuously small word with great impact on the quality of communication. Maybe now you are thinking: "But this can't be that bad!" If you think about the actual effect of the word "but", you will quickly see the problem. Picture a colleague in a heated meeting telling you "I understand where you are coming from, but..." and continuing only to explain his perspective. What is he actually saying? The truth is, he is saying: "I don't understand you", maybe even "I don't want to understand you." An expression like "You're right, but..." actually means: "You are not right and I am getting ready to explain to you why I am the one who is right." First and foremost, the word "but" signals resistance and has a crushing effect on everything that was said before. All in all, "but" has a destructive effect on the conversation and its quality, it separates instead of uniting.

Maybe now you ask yourself: "If I'm not supposed to say «but» anymore, then what can I say instead when I disagree?"

There is a very elegant alternative you can use to express your objections while preserving the relationship. It does take some rethinking. However, it is ideal to maintain the high quality of a conversation and act in a de-escalating way even when opinions differ. Instead of saying "Yes, but" you simply say "Yes, and". For example, instead of saying: "I understand, but …", you simply say: "I understand and at the same time, I can only offer you this option right now." Or you pause after the first statement and then continue: "I understand. At the moment, I only see this option." I am sure you already realize: On the emotional level, this approach has an entirely different effect.

"Yes, and" means: "Yes, you are right, and I am right as well. I understand what you are saying, I understand your anger." The statement remains what it is. This includes confirming that you consciously perceived and respect your conversation partner's opinion. "I truly understand. And, at the same time, I have a different opinion."

I want to inspire and encourage you to ban the word "but" from your vocabulary and consistently replace it with "and". Of course, your basic attitude is pivotal. If you only replace words, you will merely attain marginal effects in the long run and miss out on exploiting the full potential of improving the quality of communication. "But" slows down, blocks and creates resistance – "and" unites and keeps conversations flowing. So, are you a conversation booster or a conversation breaker?

Examples of other irritating expressions are: "You misunderstood what I said." This equals pointing your finger at someone else saying: "You made a mistake. If you had listened better, you would have understood what I said." On a factual level that is fine – on the interpersonal level, though, it is a subtle accusation. Instead, say "I think we have a misunderstanding". That leaves open who is to blame. Or if you want to take responsibility for it, you can say: "I believe I did not express myself well or: "I did not make myself clear enough." The same applies to saying "You are wrong" or "You have the wrong perspective". In that case, you are basically pointing at someone else, which disrupts or irritates the relationship.

The following statement serves as a last example: "That's not possible!" Let's assume you have a customer in front of you with a request. She has very specific expectations of how something needs to be handled and now you tell her: "No, that will not work. We can't do that." This is a nice example of problem orientation or problem focus: You talk about what is not possible because the focus of your attention lies on that. If instead, you take on a solution-focused attitude, your answer may be entirely different and you might say: What I can offer you right now is this or that." You don't talk about what is not possible, but instead point out what is. Solution orientation versus problem orientation – once again, a matter of attitude.

Listen

Interestingly, when hearing the word "communication", most people think of speaking, the active exchange of information. Only few people spontaneously first think of listening, the receiving part of communication. In their minds, people are quicker to think of the sender (the person talking), rather than the recipient (the person listening). However, listening is one of the most crucial abilities that make good communication possible in the first place. When it comes to establishing and preserving relationships and entering into real, authentic contact with others, then listening is among the most important things we can do.

Listening is also one of the most frequently neglected abilities and one of those actions in communication and interaction with other people that are the least truly consciously performed and utilized. Particularly executives who fail to listen risk being, at some point, surrounded by people who no longer have anything to say.

Thankfully, real, authentic listening is a skill that can be acquired. As is the case with many other things mentioned in this book, it is mainly a matter of attitude. You may already be familiar with the term "active listening". You have heard it before somewhere, during communication training or maybe even at school.

There is a lot more to active listening than it being just a communication technique. First of all, it describes a certain attitude – one which involves truly being able to and wanting to see the world from someone else's perspective. Looking at it this way, active listening is the most natural thing in the world and something you often do automatically. For example, if you are meeting your best friend for dinner and you have not seen each other in a while, you simply share with each other what has been happening in the past weeks and months. Maybe your friend has something on his or her heart and wants to discuss it with you. Then it is the most natural thing in the world for you to actively listen.

Predominantly, active listening pursues three main objectives:

1. Sincerely wanting to grasp what the other person wants to tell you
2. Letting the other person know that you are listening. Maintain eye contact and nod while the other person is speaking. That doesn't have to mean that you agree with what is being said, it primarily means that you are listening and in receiving mode
Wanting to understand where the other person stands and where he or she is coming from with his or her views, on a relationship level and on an emotional level. This includes hearing what is not expressed with words

This subject can become more demanding when you are forced to have a conversation you actually don't want to have, for example with someone you don't like. It might even be a conversation that makes you uncomfortable and one that you really do not feel like having. It could also be a conflict talk or a conversation where you expect there to be the possibility of conflict arising. All those factors can make sincere, active listening and taking on the corresponding attitude very challenging.

This is why active listening predominantly stands out when it does not take place – e.g. when your conversation partner avoids eye contact, thereby signaling his lack of interest, checking his smartphone instead or looking over your shoulder to scan the room for people who might be more interesting to talk to than you. That kind of behavior stands out in a negative way and has an unfavorable effect on the quality of the interaction and communication.

The intention, the motive behind listening is the decisive factor. Particularly in the business world, I often witness people listening to others only with the intention of wanting to be able to give the best possible answer when it is their turn, wanting to reply well, or rebut what the other person is saying, or, merely wanting to be quick-witted in their response. This intention is competitive and does not promote communication and good relations as it divides the parties instead of uniting them and building bridges. Along with the current trend in society which puts self-presentation first I increasingly observe conversations in which everyone only talks about themselves. A conversation may take place, but each individual only talks about him- or herself, presenting themselves in the most favorable way. This kind of conversation is not what true dialogue is all about.

No matter whether we talk about leadership, collaboration or customer contact – it is always about relationships. Listening is one of the most fundamental skills required to establish contact with others and develop as well as cultivate relationships with others. Therefore, I would like to encourage you to become even better at listening than you already are. For most of us, there is so much potential for improving the way we listen. Every individual is able to contribute to improving the quality of relationships and conversations.

The Power of Silence

In the context of listening, there is a nice play on words with the term «listen»: The same letters – L, I, S, T, E, N – can be used to spell out a different word that is directly related to the qualities of true listening. So, ... can you think of it? You will find the solution in the foot note.[25]

Silence. This term not only describes being absolutely quiet for a while – and giving others the opportunity to share their thoughts or feelings. It also pertains to the inner silence within your head while you listen: remember the story with the professor and the monk? Is your cup really "empty"? Is your mind quiet and in "idle" mode while you listen, or is it at least holding back? Are you able to tune down the volume of your own thought noise, all the noise your mind produces, in order to fully listen to your counterpart? Or are you already shifting gears, with your foot on the gas pedal, and with your mind already working on your response – while the other person is still talking? That is not the kind of silence that is required for you to be able to really listen properly.

Again, this shows the direct correlation of self-awareness and self-management: Can you manage to give the statements of your counterpart a higher priority than the results of your continuously working mind?

As is the case with listening, silence often gets underestimated and neglected when we look at communication. We tend to focus on what is being said – we focus on the words, the statements, what we hear – and, while doing so, we neglect consciously noticing the gaps between what is said: The silence in a conversation.

"Music is the space between the notes."
CLAUDE DEBUSSY[26]

Maybe now you think: "Well, yes, but... (did you really just think "but"?) silence is nothing more than the absence of noise. There is nothing special about it." Let's take a closer look at how, to take an example, music works with silence: The space between the notes is in fact one of the strongest elements influencing the character and quality of a piece of music. Even this book does not only consist of letters and words, but also of the space between them: Asentencewithoutthesespaceswouldbemuchhardertoread.

The same is true for verbal communication. The pauses between words and sentences have an effect that goes well beyond their structuring function. Basically, silence, is just space. Consequently, if silence is more than just the absence of noise and if the pauses between sentences are more than just absence of speech, then we can approach this aspect of communication in a different way.

Silence has great influence on communication in two respects. On the one hand you can use silence to emphasize your statements. Let's say you are giving a presentation which encompasses various core messages that you want to convey. Then you can do something in the spoken word which equals underlining something or putting it in bold print in writing: You add silence – following your most important message, you don't keep talking, but you add silence instead. Stop talking. Deliberately and purposely.

Say what you have to say. Put your core messages into three to four sentences, and then add silence. This automatically gives your message more weight, because you refrain from practically swiping it away with the next sentence. The principle is:

Too much information kills the information and leads to miscommunication.

If you talk nineteen to the dozen and just won't stop, your listeners will reach a point where they will no longer know what the essence of what you had to say was and what was just meant as decoration and filling material. So, utilizing silence as an active element can lead to more clarity. Interesting in this context is the issue of "fillers" or "throat-clearing sounds" or "interjections"[27] in a presentation. We have all heard them. The familiar words and sounds between sentences that usually sound like this: "Ahem, ahem" *coughing*, "mmmh, yeah, well".

Those kinds of "words" are completely useless and, to be honest, they really don't sound very intelligent. Why do we use them? Why do we use fillers between two sentences?

It is related to the fact that most people have a hard time enduring pauses while speaking or when someone else is speaking. We perceive silence as something negative. We tend to bridge silence by filling the gaps with very primitive sounds. "Ahem."

Therefore, the best way to break the habit of using fillers is not to try to stop using them, but instead befriending silence. This works best by attributing silence with a new quality by not just considering it to be the absence of noise but instead gaining an understanding of silence as an element you can actively integrate into your communication. If, by doing so, you succeed in experiencing silence as something valuable, you will automatically stop using fillers. Go ahead and try it. It works.

In conversations, your influence as far as how much silence you can add to a statement is obviously limited. After all, your counterpart can respond any time, thus breaking the silence. The moment you can use to add silence, however, is, when your conversation partner is done talking. This means you continue the silence you ideally have cultivated internally while the other person was still speaking and let it carry on externally, beyond the other person's statement. Instead of answering immediately, just purposefully wait three or four seconds. Maybe you can simply say: "Ah, yes", providing more space before you answer. Instead of pure silence you can alternatively repeat the last key word your counterpart used, or give an acoustic nod, e.g. by saying "hm …" By doing so, conversations generally do get slowed down — which usually leads to the conversation quality being perceived as being better. This brings several advantages:

First of all, you are clearly signaling: "I listened to every word you said and I allow what you said to sink in before I give you an answer. Because I take you seriously."

Secondly: You provide space and the opportunity for your conversation partner to add something to his statement and continue talking. Just like the last drop of a good bottle of red wine — which the French call "Les Amours", the love of wine. The last thing that gets said can be similarly valuable and augment the conversation by giving it more depth — because it would not have been added without the silence that provided the opportunity. This is particularly true for conversations in a leadership and customer context.

The One Who Asks Is The One Who Leads

Questions are the most efficient tool to get attention in a conversation and thereby steer its direction. The best known concept in this regard is probably the one of open and closed questions. The difference between the two can be easily understood — still, in daily operations, I often see that the tendency to ask closed questions is much higher in most people than the tendency to ask open ones.

Open questions

Open questions usually begin with words such as "who", "what", "why", or "how". If one doesn't want to be impolite, open questions require a sentence as an answer. They are ideal to establish contact, obtain information and find out more about motives. They help in keeping a conversation alive and in inspiring someone who is rather reserved to talk. A typical example: "How do you feel about this morning's meeting?"

Closed questions

They are also called «decision» questions. Typically, a closed question can only be answered with "yes" or "no". It creates commitment because it requires taking a stand. It can be used to round off a conversation. A typical example: "Did you find this morning's meeting to be productive?"

As you can see in the example, many questions can be asked in an open as well as in a closed way. What is more conducive depends on the situation and the objectives you have set for the conversation.

Special Case «Why»

In the context of open questions, there is one word which has to be used with caution due to its tendency to – depending on the situation – easily sound reproachful: The word "why". Picture the following situation: The sales director calls the salesperson into his office and asks: "Why were the numbers not achieved last month?" Depending on the tone and body language, this question can take on a reproaching and even threatening character. If the situation and relationship are already tense, this can have an escalating effect on the conversation. Again, there is no fundamental right or wrong. Instead, the question is: As a sales director, what is your goal in this situation? Don't you care about whether your salesperson is intimidated or feels offended? Or are you interested in resolving the situation in a dialogue and discussing necessary measures? Then it makes sense to act in a de-escalating manner and create a trustful atmosphere for the conversation.

What to ask if not "why"?
Well, there are valuable alternatives. Picture the sales director asking the question this way: "What led to the numbers not being achieved last month?"
Can you hear and feel the difference to the first question? It sounds much less reproachful and is thus much more de-escalating.

A few other alternatives to the classic "why" are:
// What were the decisive factors for ... ?
// How did this come about ...?

// What preceded this …?
// What caused you to …?
// How did you reach …?
// What circumstances caused …?
// Etc.

You see: There is a plethora of alternatives with which you can steer the focus of attention by how you ask the questions and be more precise than by simply asking «why».

Another step in de-escalation: Add a preliminary question to eliminate even more pressure from the conversation. "What do you think – what led to the numbers not being achieved last month?" Can you feel the de-escalating effect compared to the first question?

In the end, it is all a matter of handling questions in a careful and well-balanced manner. Closed questions exert more pressure than open ones. Short questions feel more harassing than longer questions. The shorter the breaks between individual questions are, the more intimidating the situation becomes (interrogation). Preliminary questions such as "What do you think?" or "What would you say?" reduce the pressure. The repeated use of the word "why" adds additional pressure to a conversation. Use alternatives.

Either way: By asking for reasons – even when avoiding the word "why" – you potentially invite the other person to give you explanations and justifications. This means you put the focus of the talk on the problem and its causes. Should you wish to focus on potential solutions instead and turn the conversation around, try using other, solution-focused questions instead: What can we do now? What do you think should happen next? What should it be like instead? Etc.

Likewise, I often hear people asking me a question, followed by another question, followed by yet another or even two more questions. In one sentence, that is. That has me thinking: "Well, okay then. Which question should I answer first?" So, please: Only ask one question at a time. And should you feel the strong desire to immediately ask the next question – please hold it back. Maybe your counterpart just needs a moment to give you an answer. This thought process should not be interrupted. This is of great importance for the quality of a conversation.

It means: Think about what it is that you would like to ask, ask your question and then be quiet. Even if you have to wait longer for the answer than you would wish.

Don't follow up, don't add more questions. Allow the thought process to take place, give it space, so that the other person is able to think and subsequently answer. Once again, this is a matter of enduring silence.

The same is true for your own answers when you are asked a question. In order to communicate more directly and get straight to the point, make it a habit to do the following: Take a moment to think about the following questions: What is the question I was just asked? What is it that my conversation partner wants to know from me? Then, in about three to a maximum of four sentences, answer only that question. By doing so, you will avoid boring your conversation partner with excessive answers. If instead, you provide brief and concise answers, your counterpart will ask a follow-up question, if any additional information is desired.

Attitude Altitude

I often experience how people hope for a quick "fix" of their interpersonal problems through communication techniques and methods. Executives frequently ask: "Which technique can I use to assert myself or hold my ground better? What kind of methods make me more quick-witted? What can I do to become better at influencing others?" These kinds of questions and the underlying desire to increase self-efficacy are understandable. Nonetheless, they fall short because they remain on the behavioral level and thus at the surface of what is going on.

Of course, techniques and methods play an important part in communication. It is highly valuable for you to know what kind of options you have in a conversation with high conflict potential in order to avoid escalation or to even de-escalate. However, despite all the methodology, you will not succeed in doing so if you lack the right attitude. The attitude you have regarding a conversation shows in every word and sentence you say. It influences the quality of your questions and your listening and thereby the quality of the entire communication.

Thankfully, there are some recommendations regarding the attitude to take on that have consistently proven to be conducive to good communication. They are perceived as being more far-reaching than any conversation techniques and increase the quality of leadership, cooperation and customer contact.

1. Reversibility

Could you accept what you are about to say without feeling hurt if your conversation partner was to tell you the same thing? If the answer is "no", then it might be helpful to think it over and rephrase it in a way that is less straining for the relationship.

2. Symmetry

One of the characteristics of a conversation on equal footing is a balanced share of speaking time. Symmetry as an attitude is possible even when the conversation setting is of an asymmetrical nature, e.g. a criticism meeting in a leadership context. Still, some conversations are always asymmetrical. If, for example, you are stopped by the police in the middle of the night and the officer tells you to show him your papers, then you better subordinate yourself simply based on the nature of your role. In the past, even conversations with a doctor used to be asymmetrical. Nowadays, those conversations tend to take place at eye level.

3. Authenticity

This is about being genuine and vulnerable. The prerequisite for that is a conversation climate in which you can express what you think and feel without being afraid - and without worrying about negative consequences. Do you display the person you are – even when you happen to be in a certain role, e.g. as an executive – or do you mask your behavior? Authenticity creates contact and trust, masking creates mistrust and distance. The most common masks in conversations are attack, accusation and victimization. Ultimately, they all serve the purpose of self-protection. Whether you are authentic or not mainly shows in your body language. It has a stronger effect than what you say when you are not authentic and is then perceived as inconsistent. Authenticity does not mean that you say everything you think and feel. What you say should be in line with your inner conviction, though.

4. Empathy

Surely you are familiar with the term "empathy". It stands for the ability and willingness to put yourself in someone else's shoes and look at the world from his perspective. In behavior, empathy is displayed through partner-centered questions and authentic, active listening – a behavior which you show naturally, for example when sitting on a bench and talking with your best friend. It can become more challenging when you are facing a yelling customer/employee/superior. The ability to be empathetic alone then does not suffice. In those moments, what it takes is the willingness to put yourself in the other person's position in order to make empathetic – and thus dialogue promoting – behavior possible.

5. Credibility

You are trustworthy when you follow through with what you promise, and if you only demand of others what you would demand of yourself. Part of that is having a clear understanding of the context and objective of a conversation and standing by what you said or promised.

6. Respect and Benevolence

The general willingness to respect your counterpart and his individual character does not imply that everything he says and does is to be accepted. Rather, respect and benevolence define the attitude with which you demonstrate your readiness to resolve issues in a way that does not leave a winner and a loser, but instead lets both parties win.

7. Solution Focus

When dealing with situations and challenges, you can take a problem or a solution-focused approach. A problem-oriented approach often focuses on why something happened and who is to blame, which makes it predominantly backward-looking. A solution-focused attitude focuses on potential ways to resolve the issue, which makes it future oriented. In a conversation, you can lead your conversation partner away from the problem and towards potential solutions by asking questions: "What do you think should happen next? What can we do? What do you suggest?"

No matter how well you know a technique or method – nothing can replace these basic attitudes. Even more importantly: Without the appropriate attitude, most techniques and methods are ineffective to a great extent. Therefore, the journey to better, more conflict-free communication begins by looking at yourself.

What kind of basic attitudes do you have – at work, and at home? Which of your attitudes foster conversation, which are obstructive?

RELATIONSHIP MANAGEMENT
///

In the chapter "Self-Exploration", I used the image of an iceberg to illustrate the large subconscious part that influences our behavior at the surface. Imagine what happens when two of those icebergs meet. Both controlled by mostly unconscious values, beliefs and needs, with their perception shaped by their individual filters. You can already tell that this adds significantly to the complexity of interpersonal interaction. This kind of interaction always takes place on at least two levels:

// On the *factual level*, above the surface, we experience visible behavior, spoken words, arguments, facts and content.
// On the *relationship level*, beneath the surface, we experience everything that, for the most part, takes place unnoticed on an interpersonal level.

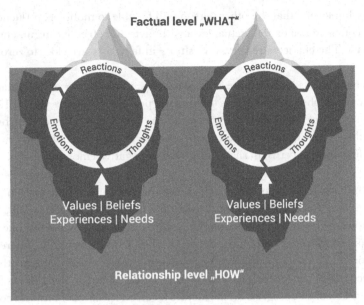

Factual level „WHAT"

Reactions

Emotions

Thoughts

Values | Beliefs
Experiences | Needs

Reactions

Emotions

Thoughts

Values | Beliefs
Experiences | Needs

Relationship level „HOW"

Image 11: The Iceberg of Interaction

In central European cultures, we tend to focus on the factual level when it comes to business operations. That even shows in the choice of words: "We want to foster factual interaction", "Let's stay with the facts", "Let's take a look at the facts ...". That is totally fine, important and correct in order to make progress in reaching targets – under one condition: That the other part, the one beneath the surface, does not get neglected, ignored, or even consciously suppressed. However, this is often the case.

It is like a real iceberg that floats in the sea and is exposed to various influences: There are winds that blow against the tip of the iceberg, maybe even storms. At the same time, there are strong currents beneath the water surface. So, what is it that actually shifts the iceberg? What determines the direction in which it moves? Is it the winds blowing against the tip? Or is it the currents below the surface? Obviously, it is the currents. The same is true for interpersonal interaction and exertion of influence: It is the relationship level that truly counts. That is the main stage on which the quality of the interaction is determined.

You have probably been in a situation in which someone tried to convince you of something – a sales person, a supervisor, a colleague, whoever. And maybe you decided early on, for yourself: "No. Not with you. No way." That means you built up inner resistance and thereby closed the door on the relationship level. Now, how likely is it in such a situation – in which you have gone into resistance on the relationship level – that the other person will be able to mobilize, influence and finally convince you on the factual level with facts and objective arguments. You guessed it: The chances are very, very slim – in fact, they are close to zero.

In other words: As long as there are disruptions, irritations or other obstacles in the way which obstruct our access to the other person, it becomes very difficult to make any progress and reach objectives on the upper factual level. Maybe even impossible. This includes unexpressed resistance and irritation, hurt feelings, anger, fear and concerns, in short: Any kind of negative emotion.

A concrete example: Picture yourself sitting in a meeting. There are ten people sitting at the table. You are in a discussion, the meeting is going well, but at some point, someone says something in a way that personally offends one of the participants. He might feel hurt, doubted, or not taken seriously. There is an irritation on the relationship level. You can imagine what kind of impact that has on the course of the meeting and the quality of the exchange that follows. If this doesn't get resolved, progress on the factual level, on the level of business content, can be compromised tremendously.

The relationship has to be the priority – above the facts. As long as there are unresolved irritations and disturbances on the relationship level, it is very difficult to reach good results on the factual level. In a nutshell: Addressing irritations has priority if you want to make effective progress on the factual level.

The Significance Of Emotions In Relationships

We make most of our decisions subconsciously and based on emotions. It is only in retrospect that we provide rational reasons, explanations and justifications for them. I am not just referring to major decisions such as making a purchase or signing a contract. This is also true for all the small decisions we make from moment to moment. In a conversation with a superior, customer or colleague, for instance, we constantly make decisions: "Do I want to keep listening? Am I still interested? Do I still have a positive attitude regarding this conversation? Or do I reach a point where I go into resistance and tell myself: ,Oh this is nonsense' or ,I would much rather be doing something else right now, I don't feel like doing this anymore.'" Those are the kind of decisions we make from moment to moment. And they greatly depend on how we feel.

> **"People will forget what you said.**
> **People will forget what you did.**
> **But people will never forget how you made them feel."**
> MAYA ANGELOU[28]

This means that how others feel in your presence and what kind of emotions you trigger in them has a much greater impact than what you say or do. In the end, what is important for the quality of a relationship is whether positive or negative emotions prevail. In order for positive emotions to appear to us as prevailing, though, you have to invest more than average due to our negative bias in perception. US-American psychologist John M. Gottman[29] speaks of a proportion of five positive interactions (compliments, appreciative statements, positive feedback) to one negative interaction (criticism, argument, sarcasm) so that relationships are generally perceived as positive. Other sources speak of a ratio of 3:1 for a working environment. Either way: It is critical for the number of positive interactions to be strongly predominant.

Establishing Contact And Building Relationships

We as humans are social beings. We were created to live in groups and support each other, even if wars and violent crimes often lead us to believe that the contrary is true. Expulsion from the group often meant certain death for our ancestors. Belonging to the group meant enjoying comfort and security. Now, particularly in western cultures, we live in a time of increasing – and in parts even excessive – individualization. The number of single households is massively on the rise and relationships have become more short-term. The "me" takes the center stage, which becomes clearly visible in the selfie culture. At the same time, though, it also shows how much we thirst for recognition, acceptance, and a sense of belonging despite our desire for individuality. In other, more collective societies, like in many Asian regions, individualization is not as pronounced yet, but it is on the rise there as well, especially among younger generations.

However, if we want to seriously achieve something together, whether it is with employees, colleagues, customers, or with our friends and families, then we need real, authentic contact. It takes warmth and empathy. This, in turn, requires the necessary awareness of the fact that we will not succeed without the willingness to reach out and approach others.

When we think about establishing relationships, we quickly think of the term "networking". This principle applies: Connections only hurt those who don't have any. Also, starting to establish a network of relationships when you need it is definitely too late. Establishing relationships requires personal contact. Social networks such as Facebook, LinkedIn and many others are useful to establish and maintain contact. When it comes to establishing real relationships, though, we are not going to get around the most effective form of social media: Real interpersonal contact.

This is the reason why, despite the technological development that made a strong increase in web and video conferences possible over the last few years, there are still more than enough situations that require a visit on site and a personal meeting. Often, this is actually the decisive factor for success. Even in a globalized world, nothing beats a handshake and personal interaction.

Friendliness And Respect

I previously pointed out that the tone of communication has become rougher over the last decades. This cannot only be noticed on board of airplanes, but also in companies. Being friendly or even nice in a business environment doesn't seem to have a good reputation, let alone be associated with success. Sometimes we can even gain the impression that inconsiderate and unfriendly people actually make quicker progress and are more successful. For instance, I can't imagine anyone who would describe Jack Welch, the former CEO of General Electric, as "nice". Still, Welch currently owns a fortune of around 720 million US Dollar.

Are there other ways that lead to success? Of course. There are many examples of people who have made it to the top in a friendly and respectful way. They demonstrate how treating people well eventually pays off. More kindness and respect in the business environment eventually leads to greater success for all parties involved.

Attitude = Altitude

When you are friendly towards others, good things happen: Doors open and opportunities arise. You will enjoy better relationships with your colleagues just as much as with your family and friends. And even if someone completely annoys you, maybe because he gossips or simply has a toxic impact with his statements and behavior, you can intervene in a direct and assertive, but nevertheless respectful and friendly way. In fact, this approach will most likely reward you with more success than if you were to be disrespectful, loud or offensive yourself. With kindness and respect, you increase your flight altitude!

Unfriendly behavior has an unhygienic effect and pollutes the atmosphere. Positive impulses, on the other hand, are like seeds. If you want to reap kindness and respect, plant kindness and respect. Smile and *principally* treat other people in a friendly and respectful way. By doing so, you ideally trigger a chain reaction of kindness which will come back to you like a boomerang. And yes, obviously there are some exceptions: If someone oversteps certain boundaries or if there is high urgency involved – as would be the case when evacuating a passenger airplane – then there obviously is no obligation to be friendly. Then it is no longer a matter of maintaining a relationship, then it is a matter of damage control or even life or death.

Also, keep in mind that people change. Someone who is your colleague or even subordinate today may become your superior someday. You never know how people will develop. Then suddenly, this one person becomes very important in your life and for you reaching your goals. Limiting your kindness to the people you want something from will not work in the long-run. If you take your clients out for dinner and treat them in the best possible way, only to turn around and be rude to the restaurant's service personnel, then this will backfire. Your behavior towards people you consider unimportant speaks volumes. "Off the record", assessment centers for future executives often analyze just that– for example, how the participants react at the check in counter when they are told that their room is not ready yet or when they are served scrambled eggs instead of fried eggs at the breakfast table. Decide today that you will treat all people with equal kindness and respect, no matter who they may be today.

Obviously, your friendliness has to be natural and authentic. Put-on, artificial behavior usually gets unmasked quickly by others. This means it takes more than "I will try to act friendly" – it takes true friendliness and respectful appreciation as a basic attitude. And last but not least: Be kind to yourself so that you can be kind to others. You may try to fake warm-heartedness, but you will not be perceived as warm-hearted and kind if you are not kind to yourself.

In other cultures, the picture is very different: My colleague Gabriela, who recently traveled to Bhutan for business, shared with me, that a traffic light at a busy intersection there, had recently been taken down again upon the request of the people because it took away an opportunity for them to live gestures of kindness by letting others go first. Another example I can name are the Swissair flights I experienced to Japan. While normally, after a long-haul flight, the passenger cabin looked like it had been hit by a tornado, we could easily have let new passengers board right after the passengers got off the plane in Tokyo. The cabin was so clean and tidy because every Japanese passenger took care of his trash out of respect and consideration towards others.

The First Impression Counts

You never get a second chance to make a good first impression. This is the mantra you have probably heard more than once. But what exactly does that mean? US-American psychologist Amy Cuddy[30] explains in her book *Presence* that there are essentially two things we evaluate in others upon meeting them for the first time – within a very short time, that is:

1. Can I trust this person?
2. Can I respect this person?

This means there are two main characteristics: Trustworthiness and competence. People who convey a lot of both are usually successful when it comes to building relationships. Too much kindness and warmth (trustworthiness) together with a lack of confidence is just as ineffective as high competence and a lack of trustworthiness. Interestingly, many people believe that competence is the more important factor. As a matter of fact, though, trustworthiness is the more important aspect during the initial assessment of other people. Looking at it from an evolutionary perspective, this is understandable: Whether we are able to trust someone is of greater importance for our survival.

Competence does play a vital role. However, it only gets evaluated when trustworthiness has proven to be a given. Putting too much focus on demonstrating your strengths and competencies can even backfire. This means if someone you are establishing contact with doesn't trust you, you will not get far. You may even raise the suspicion of you trying to manipulate others. A trustworthy person, radiating warmth, and also appearing competent and strong, has a much more effective impact – as only after trust has been established does this competence become a gift, rather than turning into a potential threat.

Reciprocity: The Principle Of Mutual Influence

Most of us have been to a networking event and felt what it is like to be approached by other participants and, within a matter of a few minutes, be scanned for what he or she could possibly offer the other person – only for some of those people to swiftly turn away if they don't immediately identify what that might be. Hardly anything feels more awkward than that and this approach obviously does not provide a good foundation for establishing relationships.

In order to build successful relationships, it is worthwhile to consider an important principle right from the start: The principle of reciprocity. The essence of this principle is that as human beings, we feel a strong obligation to mirror the behavior we experience. This means if someone does us a favor, we are inclined to repay this favor. This is one of the reasons why donation collectors in the streets often work with giving small presents first. Or maybe you are familiar with the free Christmas cards certain organizations send out during the Christmas season – with an enclosed deposit slip and a request for donations. These strategies are based on the principle of reciprocity: Give first – take later.

Ask yourself how you can create more value for others. What can you give others? Where can you be generous? It could be information, or simply authentic, honest compliments. What stands above everything else is authenticity. If authenticity is not given and your compliments are perceived as fake and artificial, then the scheme backfires. Become known as someone who generates added value for others. The principle of reciprocity takes care of the rest.

The same principle applies when your intention is to create interest: How do you reach that goal of others being interested in you? By talking about yourself? By sharing your achievements and how successful you have been? How great you are? You could think this is actually true, based on listening to many people. Far from it! If you want others to start showing an interest in you, then show interest in them first. Ask open questions to establish contact.

Maintaining Relationships

One major factor when it comes to maintaining relationships is how conflicts are handled – how they are prevented and how they are managed when they are acute. Both situations can be handled successfully when you are familiar with the basic principles of effective conflict management. Let me discuss these in detail below.

Individual differences between people and the uniqueness of each person can lead to a lack of understanding and tension. This tension can in turn lead to misunderstandings, distrust, rejection and ultimately conflicts – or understanding, trust, acceptance and enrichment. Whether things take a turn in one direction or the other is primarily a question of how the differences and the tension they create are handled.

The most common reasons for interpersonal conflicts are actual or perceived threats to our values, beliefs and interests and a subsequent form of inadequate or insufficient communication. That means if we don't understand another person's behavior, we basically don't understand his or her values and needs.

Even though a conflict often is something unpleasant, it can have positive sides to it. For example, a conflict can help clarify different views, standpoints and objectives. At least a conflict creates an opportunity to reach an agreement, convergence and maybe even a new joint realignment. Often, innovations emerge from conflict, e.g. when a customer is unsatisfied with a product or a service and it is only thanks to his needs being noticed that the company recognizes that their services need to be adjusted.

I like comparing conflicts with summer thunderstorms. Usually, before they happen, it is humid, the air feels heavy and unpleasant. Then the thunderstorm starts rolling in. Tension builds up – until eventually energy is released in the form of flashes of lightning, which harmonizes the atmosphere. After the thunderstorm, the air feels clear, fresh and clean again. The same is true for the situation following a resolved conflict, as long as the conflict was handled in a fair, respectful and appreciative manner. Let's not forget, a thunderstorm can also cause great damage and be as destructive as a conflict that builds up over an extended period of time, is not adequately addressed and then escalates without any control.

Put The Fish On The Table – Approaching Conflicts With Determination

This idiomatic expression vividly illustrates an important attitude when it comes to handling conflicts: Picture conflicts as dead fish lying under the table for as long as they are not dealt with. What happens when a dead fish just keeps lying under the table? What if there is even more than one and they start to pile up? They start to smell, or even stink. The air gets thick. In fact, we can sense the tension when there are conflicts in the air. Instead, put the fish on the table before it starts to smell.

When you notice one or more conflict symptoms, provide an opportunity for the other person involved to express a potential disturbance or irritation. Obviously, you should not say: "Hey, what is wrong with you?!" Instead, simply give him or her a chance to address and talk about a potential irritation: "What is your current position regarding the issue we're discussing?" Or: "How do you feel about this issue?" Or: "What do you think about this?" The important part is to stay completely neutral and refrain from making any kind of accusations.

When a conflict has reached an advanced stage and a clarifying conversation becomes necessary, then be decisive in doing so. Let's refer to this approach as "positive confrontation". Hold on – confrontation? You might wince when you read this word, and it may have a negative connotation for you. Maybe you even associate it with escalation or violence. This is quite understandable. However, let's take a look at this term's origin. It derives from the Latin word "con", which stands for "with", and "frons", which stands for "front" of "forehead". One could consequentially say "to confront" someone means "to approach" someone in order to meet "face-to-face" and collaborate in tackling and resolving a troublesome issue. Looking at it from this perspective, a new, positive image of the term "confrontation" evolves, one of two parties working towards the same goal. It expresses that, through collaboration, we strive to find a common solution in the best interest of all parties involved.

To positively influence and change the dynamics in such a situation, you can ask two simple questions. These questions allow you to turn a situation around from being oriented against each other, to one in which both parties are looking in the same direction. Instead of being face-to-face, staring into each other's eyes, these questions enable you to turn your heads in the same direction and aim for the same targets.

1. "Yes" to the situation:

Ask the other person if he or she agrees that there is indeed a disagreement or conflict between the two of you. "Do you agree that we disagree?" A "Yes, of course I share that opinion" often is the first "yes" after a long period of entrenched positions and resistances shaped by "no". A "yes" as an answer creates an initial mutual agreement and thus a first connecting element.

2. "Yes" to the commitment:

The second question is: "Are you as ready as I am to contribute your share in finding a common solution?" This question directs the attention towards the future and towards taking a joint approach. If now you get a "yes", you are no longer standing face-to-face, but are looking in the same direction. You may still be standing on your respective side of the topic, but now you have reassured each other of your willingness to do what it takes to find a solution and you are both directing your attention towards the same objective. That is something that unites.

Everyone Is Right

When it comes to managing conflicts, the underlying attitudes play a vital role: If you allow your ego to take control, and its natural striving for survival, being right and winning, that will have a different impact on the course of events than if you consciously take on a de-escalating attitude.

In this process, a viewpoint which might seem somewhat radical at first can be very helpful: "Every person is always right – from her perspective." Maybe you are acknowledging this statement with a nod right now and you are able to easily accept and take on this attitude. Now, let me ask you to go back and think about the last conflict you were involved in, one in which you were very upset and the emotions were raging high. Could you see yourself taking on this attitude in that kind of situation? And do you think this attitude would positively affect your behavior in this situation?

"I disapprove of what you say, but I will defend your right to say it to the death."
E.B. HALL[31]

"I'm okay, you're okay" is the underlying attitude that assumes that the other person acts based on his or her values, beliefs, and needs and stands up for them. This does not mean you agree with the other person's opinion. You merely grant others the right to be just as convinced of being right as you believe to be right in this particular moment. You can continue to say "no" to the facts and the conflict itself, while saying "yes" to the person and thus to the relationship you share. If you manage to enter the conversation with this attitude, the interpersonal interaction will take on a completely different nature than if you were to enter with the attitude "I am right and you are wrong. And now I am going to prove it to you!" This way, it is no longer a question of who is right. Instead, it becomes a question of what is best for the situation.

By taking such a cooperative approach, you maintain contact and stay in touch with the other person, despite things being challenging on the content level. This has a de-escalating effect and thus a positive impact on the further development of the interaction. Attacking the other person, on the other hand, only creates an additional problem which not only distracts from the conflict itself, but also additionally complicates the entire situation and makes finding a solution more difficult. In comparison, an attitude of "I'm not okay – You're okay" in most cases leads to withdrawal and discontinuation, one of "You're not okay – I'm okay" to alienation and one of "I'm not okay – You're not okay" to hardened fronts and an end of the discussion.

I believe that the following Zen story describes the attitude I just explained very well:

Once upon a time, there was a fisherman who had just finished giving his boat a new coat of paint. He was very happy with the new shine he had given it. And so he decided early in the morning to go for a short ride, despite the water still being covered by a thick coat of fog. After he had been out on the water for quite a while, all of a sudden, he was hit by another boat that had appeared out of nowhere. The thud had scared him so much that he almost fell overboard, but his growing anger prevented him from falling. He cussed and raged. How could someone be so careless and scratch the surface of his newly painted boat!

But then he realized that there was no one in the other boat. It was empty. There was no other person who had intentionally hit him, there was no one who wanted to hurt him on purpose. Once he reached the shore, he was still a little upset about what had happened. But when the last thought of someone obviously having tied up the boat not well enough had faded, he began to laugh out loud. How ridiculous was it, to get upset about an empty boat.

With a few exceptions, the boats we get upset about usually are empty – and we only suspect someone in them who deliberately wants to hurt us. Recognizing that makes it easier to say "no" to the issue and "yes" to the person. This may even enable you to assume the other person has the best intentions. Based on this assumption, how would you then behave in a conflict – as the best version of yourself?

Creating Space To Break Reactive Patterns

Who has not wished someone else would change? You have probably had this wish more than once – and you are not the only one. At the same time, we all know how unlikely it is for an adult person to change only because we have that wish. However, in conflict situations, our logical demand is for just that to happen: We want the other person to change, or at least change his or her standpoint.

By doing so, we often find ourselves in reactive patterns we share with others. In other words: You behave and communicate in a certain way, the other person reacts to your behavior, you in turn react to the other person's behavior, which in turn leads to your counterpart reacting.... And so you are both trapped in a reactive pattern. In the worst case, the whole dynamic is of bad nature, loaded with conflict, and neither of you manages to break the pattern. Even worse: Each of you is just waiting for the other person to finally change. In the worst case, you are both standing in a sort of emotional fog which causes you to react with your habitual and unconscious reactive patterns. This can go on and on over the course of weeks, months, or even years.

Where is the lever for the change we long for in our conversation partner, business partner, boss, customer, colleague, life companion? Well, the lever obviously lies within us. We cannot force anyone to change his or her behavior towards us. However, we can efficiently invite others to change their behavior by changing ours.

First of all, it takes awareness in order to break such a pattern. For one thing, you need to be aware of what takes place within you, what kind of buttons the other person is pushing in you and what kind of patterns and automatic reactions that triggers in you. Then, you need to be aware of what takes place during the interaction between you and the other person. If you are as attentive as you need to be and notice what takes place in you as well as in the interaction with your counterpart, then you need to create the space that is required to replace your autopilot mode with consciously chosen and de-escalating behavior. A proven formula to create the necessary space in conflict-ridden conversations, is **STIR**. It stands for:

STop! – **I**nhale – **R**espond

Make it a habit to take one or two conscious breaths, particularly when you find yourself in a strongly emotional situation. By doing so, you create the space in which you can consciously choose your response: "How can I behave in a de-escalating relationship-oriented way and lead both of us, as mutual partners, out of this reactive pattern?" It is even possible that, in this process, you decide not to respond at all.

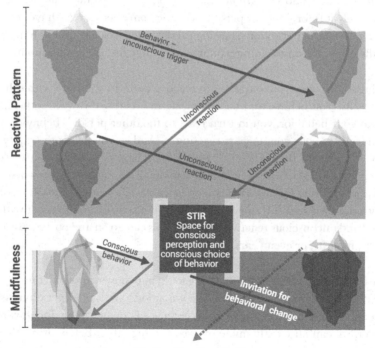

Image 12: Breaking Reactive Patterns

The consciously chosen behavior must not necessarily bring fundamental change. Often, the smallest modifications in your choice of words, your tone, or your attitude are what leads to the desired change in others. For example, you can decide to consciously listen more and more closely – that entails truly listening, being authentic in how you listen, with the intention of truly gaining a better understanding of what the other person is expressing, instead of the intention of coming up with the best possible answer or being able to rebut what your counterpart is saying.

Alternatively, you can consciously decide to summon up a greater understanding of your counterpart's position and to demonstrate this by expressing it in words. This leads to a small, yet fundamental change in your behavior. Subsequently, there is a high probability for your counterpart to show the change you desire, simply based on you inviting him or her to adjust to your new attitude.

When you encounter understanding instead of resistance and rejection during a conflict resolution talk, when you experience a conversation with someone who sincerely listens to you and understands your position – how does that make you feel? Do you still feel you have to vigorously defend your position like you did before? Or are you possibly able to break down your walls and show greater understanding for the other person who is inviting you to build bridges and enter into a dialogue?

Creating the necessary space can also mean refraining from immediately answering an email you find particularly outrageous, insulting and offensive. Instead, you allow for some time to pass, a few hours, maybe, or even an entire day and answer the email after the world has rotated once around its axis. You may then end up choosing a different communication channel because you realize that it is time to seek a personal conversation.

Keep making yourself aware of the lever for change: It is in your hands, not in the hands of your counterpart. If you desire change in the other person, then think about the following: What can I do to invite the other person to change his or her behavior? This simple rule applies: If what you are doing has the desired effect – that is, if the impact that you notice is headed in the right direction - then do more of it. If what you are doing does not lead to the desired change in the other person's behavior, then try something different. Until you are able to get your foot in the door. And then do more of that.

Often, all it takes is for one of the parties involved to remain attentive and aware in order to make a difference. However, there is no guarantee. Human beings are complex systems and you cannot always count on the other person finishing what you started. Obviously, there are many other factors that affect the situation. Still, the probability that something will change is high as long as you are attentive and make a conscious decision to work on changing your behavior and pave the way towards true dialogue and constructive collaboration.

The Aikido Principle

The idea that our attention functions as a fertilizer for everything we direct it to, allowing it to grow and gain momentum, particularly when it is something negative, is especially true when it comes to conflict situations because then our tendency to evaluate and perceive statements as well as behaviors as being "negative", is even greater. It is usually during times when we have problems or are worried about something that our thoughts tend to revolve around our problems. Often, we reach a state we could call "problem trance", which we cannot manage to escape from.

In a difficult conversation, what do you direct your attention to – and, through the way you ask your questions, where do you direct the focus of your conversation partner? Is it towards the problems, differences and issues, or towards solutions and options? How can you handle a conversation that is shaped by negativity and resistance in a solution-focused way? What do you do when your counterpart is stuck in problem trance, complains, whines or even verbally attacks you?

In these cases, you can revert to tools used in martial arts, in which the objective is to resolve conflicts. As an example, I would like to highlight Aikido which originated in Japan. It offers some helpful principles which can easily be applied in conflict talks:

1. Do not put up any resistance against the energy of the enemy's attack. Do not go against it
2. No attack, no counterstrike
3. Redirect your opponent's attack, by reverting his energy

Transferring these principles to the context of conversations shaped by negativity, attacks, complaints etc. can be very helpful as well: Not going against or resisting what you are facing, e.g. by saying "Yes, but ...". Instead, go along with what is coming your way and redirect it: Away from the problem focus into solution-orientation. This can be best achieved by asking future and solution-focused questions. Here are some examples:

// "What do you suggest?"
// "What should we do now?"
// "What are your expectations?"
// "What should it be like instead?"
// "In your opinion, what should be different?"
// "What do you plan on doing to change that?"

// "What have you already done to change that?"

By asking these kinds of questions, you invite your conversation partner to step away from the problem focus — and a potential problem trance — and step into solution-orientation. There are countless alternatives and obviously, not all the questions are appropriate for all potential situations. Rather, the important thing is that you take on the right attitude and, instead of allowing yourself to be pulled into a reactive pattern, consciously redirect the focus of the conversation.

Managing Highly Emotional Reactions

In case a conflict still escalates, you need to de-escalate it. In order to be able to do so, you need to learn to effectively handle your own emotions as well as those of the people involved in the conflict. Strong reactions are often shown when a certain kind of behavior or an event triggers strong emotions, that is, is someone is "pushing our buttons". In these situations, it is particularly important to stay in contact with the other person and yourself, put your ego on a leash and be empathic in order to de-escalate the situation.

Make yourself aware of the fact that the person showing such a fierce and emotional reaction is covered by dense emotional fog which gravely limits his or her ability to hear or accept rational arguments such as "Just calm down now" (see previous chapter: "The Valley Of Tears"). If you want to help this person to deal with this distorted perception, to regain clarity and provide support in the process, simply follow these rules:

1. Acknowledge the emotional reaction.
2. Show understanding.
3. Ask open questions regarding the other person's needs.
4. Wait until the other person has calmed down before you use rational arguments to clarify the situation.

In order for you to be able to act as described above, it is important that you do not perceive the emotional reaction you are facing as something negative or even as a threat. Always keep in mind that your counterpart is reacting this way based on feeling that their values, beliefs or needs are actually or allegedly threatened.

If a conversation still threatens to escalate because both rationally thinking brains were just hijacked by emotions it can make sense to interrupt and adjourn the conversation — for a few hours or longer, until the emotions have subsided and a rational conversation is possible again. Ideally, recognize your own needs and use

I-statements, for example by saying: "I notice that I am highly emotional right now and it is very important for me that we are able to speak to each other in an appreciative and respectful manner. Therefore, I am requesting a break in our conversation."

///

STOPOVER - WE

Use your own words to summarize what you have learned for yourself in this last chapter and what kind of information you consider to be the most important or helpful for you.

_____

_____

_____

_____

_____

_____

_____

_____

Think about the findings you would like to transfer to your professional or personal life. What kind of intentions have already begun to take root and where do you see opportunities to put them into practice?

_____

_____

_____

_____

_____

_____

_____

_____

///

PRE-FLIGHT (PART 2)

///

Continued from page 16 ...

Directly and without hesitation, I walked up to the man, opened my arms with my palms pointing forward and, as calmly as possible, said to him in English: "Sir, I see that you are very upset. I am the person responsible. Talk to me. I will listen to you!" He started to insult me as well and wanted to know who I was. I repeated my statement and because I noticed that there were four empty middle seats close to us, I suggested that we sit down so we could talk in peace.

He seemed to calm down a little and accepted my suggestion. So we sat down next to each other in the empty middle row and I started the conversation by asking him where he was from. He said he had just come from Karachi (Pakistan) and was on his way to visit family in Frankfurt. Then he began to talk badly about the political system of the country of his origin. I no longer remember all the things he said, but he was truly in a rage. Still, he appeared to be sober. I sat with him, allowed him to talk and listened to him, while I continued to consciously convey my understanding. Out of the corner of my eye, I saw a flight attendant and gave her a nod to reassure her of me having everything under control at the moment. I assumed that the cabin crew had informed the cockpit crew in the meantime and was keeping them updated.

The atmosphere in economy class was noticeably tense and the crew did its best to carry out the on-board service in a normal way on this – thankfully short – flight. We were just about to go into descent, when the supposed peace was suddenly over again and the passenger started yelling again. He yelled at me, telling me to go away and that he wanted to talk to someone else now. I was friendly, but determined, when I told him that I would allow him to talk to one of my female colleagues only under one condition: He would have to guarantee me that he would remain quiet for the rest of the flight and refrain from yelling or even threatening anyone for the rest of the flight. He promised to comply and I told him I would find out if one of my colleagues was willing to sit down next to him.

I got up and walked back to the economy galley. Once there, I told the flight attendants who were making all the preparations for landing what was going on and asked them if one of them was willing to sit with the passenger until we landed. The three of them looked at each other and Brigitte, the youngest among them, said she would do it. We walked back to the passenger together. He had indeed sat quietly in his seat in the meantime, only grumbling to himself.

"This is my colleague Brigitte", I said. "She will sit next to you for the rest of the flight. I expect you to treat her with respect and not give us any trouble. Will you promise me that?" I intentionally spoke loud enough for the passengers sitting in the rows around us to be able to hear me. I looked at Brigitte and asked her again if this was truly alright for her. She nodded and took the seat next to him. I consciously sought eye contact with some other passengers and received affirmative looks by which they reassured me of their support.

I went straight to the flight deck. As expected, the pilots had already been informed that there was a problem with a passenger. I gave them my assessment of the situation and we agreed to call the police for our arrival in Frankfurt. At that time, we did not know whether the officers would receive the passenger when he got off the plane or take him into custody directly from his seat.

I walked to the back of the plane again to check on the situation and everything appeared to be calm and quiet. The Pakistani passenger was engaged in a conversation with my colleague and seemed to act reasonably. The preparations for landing went well and since Brigitte was not assigned a door, she was able to stay with the passenger throughout the landing. Upon my inquiry, the captain confirmed that the police were waiting for us. I asked my colleagues in economy class to keep an eye on the passenger and notify me immediately should there be any more problems after we landed.

Upon arrival in Frankfurt we taxied to our assigned parking position and after the passenger bridge was docked into position, I waited for the knock which was our signal that the door could be opened. I opened the door and saw four police officers in uniform. They inquired about the situation and I confirmed that, at the moment, things were quiet. We agreed to let the passengers disembark and take the person in question into custody upon disembarkation. The other passengers left the plane calmly and when the passenger got off the plane, he showed the officers no resistance to his arrest.

Once all the passengers had disembarked from the plane, I used the intercom to call the entire crew for a debriefing. We gathered in first class and the two pilots joined us. At that moment, I needed to make sure that the entire crew were informed about what had happened and that everyone was in a balanced emotional state that allowed them to do their job on the return flight. Brigitte started to cry when I asked her how she was doing. Obviously, she had been under great pressure which could finally be relieved. After the debriefing, all the other crew members declared that they were "fit for flight" and started preparing the cabin for the return flight, while I took a moment to get some fresh air with my Brigitte.

We sat down on the steps leading up to the gangway and the sun was shining upon our faces. Neither one of us said a word. We just sat there. After a while, Brigitte said that this had been the worst thing that she had ever experienced on a flight. I gave her an affirmative nod and told her that she had been very brave and professional and how very grateful I was for that. She took a deep breath, smiled and said: "Let's fly home."

DESTINATION LEADERSHIP

///

Image 13: Destination Leadership

ABOVE THE CLOUDS

///

The leadership work onboard a passenger airplane is very unique in many ways. At the same time, it is shaped by several principles that also apply in other professional environments, in which the essence is effective leadership and the cooperation of people: Clarity and honesty. Plus communication, respect and mutual trust as well as adhering to standard operational procedures, so called SOPs.

The briefing that takes place before every flight was always a good and important opportunity for me to prepare the crew for the flight on a factual level and share the latest additional information about passenger profiles, pre-ordered special meals, passengers requiring a wheel chair service or other special issues. Part of the briefing was the emergency briefing in which existing knowledge was discussed or the most important safety aspects regarding an aircraft type and routing were called to mind.

This briefing was the only opportunity to turn a group of up to 16 crew members[32] into a team within the shortest amount of time - ideally, a team in which each person trusted the other and where everyone was willing to support their fellow crew members, committed to providing outstanding customer service. A team that would also function one hundred percent in case of an emergency. We were a team and that meant we worked together, not against each other. This was the reason why I, just like many other M/Cs, placed just as much value on providing mutual support when it came to leadership in order to ensure that the team was doing well. Whenever we as a team were not doing well any more, when we were possibly stressed or entangled in conflict with each other, it directly affected the quality of our collaboration and spread to our passengers.

The briefing was not only about reporting facts, it was just as much about establishing contact on the relationship level. It was about assessing the mood of the cabin crew members, finding out if there were any individuals who showed signs of outstanding commitment or noticeable negativity, frustration or resistance. They had to be met and picked up from where they were. Towards the end of the briefing, we were usually joined by the cockpit crew. They shared information from their perspective, e.g. regarding the weather: Do we expect a calm flight? Do we expect to experience some turbulence along the way? This provided an opportunity for the cabin and the cockpit crew to establish contact with each other prior to the flight, and it allowed them to share their expectations regarding our collaboration.

One very special aspect was how mistakes were handled. The airline industry, and particularly flight operations, are considered the pioneers of a culture that handles mistakes in a transparent way. Every single day, there are 100,000 flights taking place worldwide, transporting around two million passengers. Measured by the number of flights alone, accidents in aviation are at an all-time low and flying is in fact the safest form of transportation.

Apart from technological progress and increasingly reliable systems, the reason for that lies in the manner in which mistakes are handled. Nowhere else have I experienced such a natural, open and professional way of dealing with errors. While in many companies, mistakes are still considered to be something bad which is to be avoided, and executives lead their employees accordingly while employees live in a more or less intense fear of making a mistake, this practice has long been abolished by the airline industry. For a reason: Where people work, mistakes are made. So, instead of sanctioning mistakes, the objective has to be a candid handling of errors. Particularly in aviation, it is not the actual mistakes that lead to accidents, but the undiscovered mistakes which are repeated and, in the worst case, add up to a fatal chain of errors.

On the evening of November 14, 1990, an Alitalia DC-9 crashed into the Stadlerberg mountain as it approached the Zurich-Kloten airport. The crash – a so-called "controlled flight into terrain" – killed 46 people. One of the reasons for the crash was a malfunction of the altimeter, which caused the plane to fly about 900 ft too low, directly flying towards the mountain. The pivotal factor was a different one, though, and it turned out to have a fatal consequence: The 28 year-old co-pilot who was the one flying the approach and landing maneuver recognized the wrong altitude and – immediately and correctly – started a go-around pattern. The 47 year-old captain, however, instructed him to interrupt the maneuver and go back into descent. Two independent studies later proved that, by performing a go-around, the plane would have made it over the mountain. In the end, the unfortunately still popular dogma that the boss is always right prevailed – even though it was the co-pilot who had done what was right.

On one hand, a mistake that is covered up out of fear can turn into a much bigger and no longer controllable problem. On the other hand, a valuable opportunity to learn from it is lost. Still, even in aviation, a culture of handling mistakes transparently does not start all on its own and naturally. Instead, it has to be learned and trained. In so-called crew resource management trainings (CRM), flight and cabin crews practice talking about problems in an open and non-accusatory way. The objective is not to discuss what happened and whose fault it is, but how it could happen and what can be done to ensure that it won't happen again. The underlying attitude is completely different and can make a great difference in other companies as well.

In such a company culture, mistakes must not be punished – otherwise, there is no incentive for addressing them openly. Among other prerequisites, this requires a flat hierarchy. This is something that was already a given in our environment back then, during my time at Swissair. Of course, the captain always had full responsibility for the plane, the crew and the passengers and he or she was ultimately the highest-ranking decision maker on board. Still, the interaction took place at eye-level, and it was shaped by mutual respect, appreciation and friendliness. We called each other by our first names, which made it easier to establish contact and build as well as preserve relationships in leadership and collaboration. Distance was abolished and trust built more quickly – things that can be crucial during normal operations and in case of an emergency. There was also a feedback form on board that could be used by each crew member to provide a fellow crew member – including the captain – with feedback. Positive as well as critical, that is.

This is not the case everywhere. There are still airlines that provide a separate bus, sometimes even a limousine, that takes the cockpit crew to the aircraft, their carry-on luggage gets carried up the stairs by dedicated personnel and they get to stay at better hotels at their destinations than the cabin crew. Often, in these cultures the crew members address each other not by their first name, but the formal way.

CHALLENGES IN LEADERSHIP
///

One of the biggest challenges companies are facing is finding and retaining qualified personnel. Finding employees obviously has something to do with how attractive the company is, the offered functions and the development opportunities. Marshall Goldsmith[33] and his team interviewed more than 200 high-potentials from all over the world on the subject of retention. One key question was: "If you would like to stay with this company, what are your reasons?" Here are the top three answers:

1. "I find a sense of purpose here and job satisfaction. The work is exciting and I love what I am doing."
2. "I like the people here. They are my friends. It feels like a team – like a family. Maybe I could make more money somewhere else, but I don't want to leave the people here."
3. "I am able to fulfill my dreams. This organization allows me to grow and do what I truly want to do in my life."

This is of particular relevance for the younger generation that has been joining companies in recent years: They place greater value on development opportunities, being treated with respect and dignity and finding a sense of purpose in their work. In addition, nowadays employer review sites create a new transparency in the work market: Prior to applying, potential candidates do some research. This way, not only customers, but also employees obtain information beforehand which, in the worst case, leads to qualified employees not even sending their application to a certain company at all.

The way leadership operates has great impact on the previously mentioned factors. But how is this handled in companies? Take a look at your own experiences as an employee: Independent of whether you have been in an executive function for a longer period, are just starting your career as an executive or have never been in a leadership position, you have probably worked under various supervisors over the course of your career and experienced different leadership styles first hand. I am sure, some of your experiences with executives were good, they allowed you to experience leadership as something helpful and beneficial, you looked up to them, they inspired you and encouraged you to gain new experiences.

On the other hand, you have probably had one or two supervisors who you experienced to demonstrate negative or obstructive leadership skills. I have had several such superiors and almost everyone I talk to shares this experience: I hear many examples that evolve around a lack of appreciation, a lack of respect, a lack of trust, and not following through on promises. I hear reports about executives who say one thing and do another – or reap the benefits for what the team accomplishes, while pointing a finger at the team whenever something goes wrong.

Furthermore, a lack of presence is often mentioned: The executive is simply absent, so there is no leadership. Another example of poor leadership is micro management by a superior, that is, an executive continuously telling his or her employees what they need to do even though they would be perfectly able to know this and do it on their own – if they were only given the chance. This often gives employees the impression of being instrumentalized. They feel like they are turned into executing organs, human robots that are supposed to do as they are told and refrain from contributing their thoughts or suggestions. The supervisors believe they know better – after all, they are the supervisors.

As has been proven, nowadays only a small number of people sincerely feel a connection with their company. A much higher number of employees is either not motivated or even demotivated. The difference lies in *not motivated* employees only performing well enough not to get into trouble. They follow the "work-to-the-rule" principle. Those who are *actively demotivated* deliberately display negative behavior, spread a bad spirit, talk badly about the company and its management and actually have a toxic effect: With their active demotivation, they poison the work climate and pull others down with them.

In the eyes of the employees, many executives do an insufficient job. The often quoted statement "People apply to work for a company – and they leave their supervisors" is not only a provocation, but it is also cause for great concern because it hits the nail on the head. Far too rarely do executives give their employees enough leeway to act in an independent and committed way in the company's best interest, allowing them to make the decisions they are fully capable of making and contributing to resolving the issues that concern them the most. The potential and the competencies the employees already have in place are not utilized nearly enough.

The quality and efficiency of leadership varies greatly from company to company. What are the reasons behind this phenomenon? For one thing, many companies offer no other career path than that of assuming a leadership role. This means, many employees who desire to advance in their career and take on more responsibility – and increase their income – end up in an executive position even though that may not be what they actually want. This is different in companies that also offer a specialist's career path where employees are able to further advance in their career without taking on a leadership position.

Is Leadership Self-Evident?

In today's business world, leadership is often considered as being something that is self-evident and that some people are just better at it than others. This is a notion that is particularly wide-spread among small and medium-sized enterprises. It is also the reason why, often, those employees who are the most competent in technical terms are the ones who are entrusted with a leadership position. With this approach, the best sales person automatically turns into head of sales, or the best specialist is promoted to team leader. Experience shows, though: Being competent in their field does not make someone competent as a leader. In many cases, changing into a leadership position even comes close to switching to a new profession – when you take a closer look at the challenges that come with the new role. The importance of technical competence usually declines in the new role, depending on the industry and hierarchy level. In turn, competencies in the areas of personal, interpersonal and methodological competence become increasingly relevant. However, they are often not recognized as being important and subsequently not systematically developed.

In the worst case, this could lead to a company losing its best expert and gaining an average-performing leader who sometimes does better and sometimes worse – who increasingly becomes frustrated and unhappy. When the pressure increases, these executives often instinctively retreat back to their comfort zone which means they go back to the tasks they are competent and successful in. So, they end up running back to the playing field and scoring goals instead of supporting their team members in attaining theirs.

This also affects the satisfaction and commitment of the employees who fall under such leadership. It is obvious that someone who became supervisor under such circumstances will hardly turn into an inspiring and passionate leader, who is accepted as a role model, whom the employees follow because they want to – and not because they have to. Quite contrary, these employees experience a leader who, in their eyes, is not qualified which leads to frustration on their part and makes them feel instrumentalized and not taken seriously, so their commitment declines and, in the worst case, they leave their boss.

Crucial: The Relationship Between Leaders And Employees

Respectful and appreciative interaction as well as open, transparent communication are absolutely essential if both parties want to benefit from each other. However, reality often speaks a different language – more or less clearly, depending on the industry: In many cases, the tone is rather rough and the leadership style that the executives display varies between a lot of pressure and no pressure – depending on how an employee's performance is perceived. Things can even get loud and disrespectful, even blows below the belt are possible – which is something that definitely has no place in a modern and professional leadership approach. Whatever the specifics may be, no situation justifies disrespectful behavior. Those who lose their employees' respect ultimately lose the employees.

Disrespect comes at a high cost. Most people have experienced harsh behavior in the workplace at least once and many employees who have experienced uncivilized behavior in the workplace subsequently deliberately cut down their work effort. They spend their time trying to avoid an encounter with the respective person. Uncivilized behavior keeps people from blossoming and, worse yet, employees who are subjected to such bad behavior often end up acting in an uncivilized manner themselves.

The leaders are the ones who set the tone when it comes to what the interaction with each other is like. Just one black sheep can have great influence on the entire company culture. If employees already wince when such an executive enters the room and if they have to work under great pressure, constantly expecting to be reprimanded, the conversations during coffee breaks are not going to be positive. Instead of talking about how the company and oneself can be further developed, they will talk about how everyone can best get out of the game with minimal damage. The company culture is contagious, and employees adjust to their environment.

Many of my professional colleagues, male and female, as well as an increasing number of qualified executives and I share the firm belief that anything that takes place below a minimum of respect in professional interaction is a no-go!

Or, in other words: What could possibly give an executive the right to reprimand an employee, that is, to be totally disrespectful towards a grown-up person? No grounds on earth give someone in a leading position the right to act in such a way.

The reason for uncivilized and disrespectful behavior usually lies in a lack of alternative courses of action. The executive simply does not know how else to react to an employee not meeting the expectations regarding performance and behavior or to an employee making a mistake. It is important that we differentiate between a non-recurring "slip" and constant behavior. The desired effect is hardly ever achieved with an uncivilized approach. In addition to the toll it takes on the quality of the relationship, it comes with a massive loss of respect and acceptance. At the same time, this kind of behavior is a sign for the person in charge not seeing any other options. It is actually a demonstration of weak leadership – and the people who act this way primarily disqualify themselves.

Appreciative Leadership Increases The Company's Profitability

It may sound like a truism at first. At the same time, my practical experience shows that despite it being underlined by extensive studies and research and proven with many findings, this fact has not been recognized by all senior and top executives of companies: In the long-run, happier employees are more productive than unhappy ones. They are usually sick less often, feel less driven to leave the company and are thus more loyal, and they are even willing to go the extra mile, when necessary. On top of that, they attract other employees who are just as engaged and committed.

But what does happiness in the workplace mean? It does not mean modesty or complacency. Instead, it is about the feeling of being successful and flourishing in your own doing, in your contribution to the company's success. Looking at it from this perspective, a flourishing workforce is not only a happy one, but also one that is actively committed to their own as well as the company's future. At the same time, committed employees are experiencing positive stress without running the risk of suffering from burnout.

Particularly companies with high productivity and profitability have proven to be characterized by executives who are not only allowed to lead, but who are able and willing to lead. This is true because they possess the competencies and tools it takes to lead and they know they are in a position to fulfill their role. Among all criteria, the factor with the greatest influence on profitability is the willingness and ability of an executive to take the time to express appreciation for the employees and their development, to request and give feedback – to include expressing critique, and to foster a culture of collaboration among the employees. Part of that is the ability and the willingness to understand the personal motives, hopes and challenges of each team member. Ideally, such an executive is able to establish framework conditions and support mechanisms that allow every team member to live up to his or her full potential.

Under that kind of conditions, the employee is able to put his or her focus on the customer, which in turn has an ultimate effect on profitability. However, this development requires a cultural change: Away from instrumentalizing and utilizing employees as a pure resource (= human resources), towards an appreciative leadership culture in which developing potential, ownership and self-organization serve as the basis for collaboration (= human leadership).

Developing Leadership Competencies Must Be A Priority
It becomes obvious that the systematic development of leadership competencies is an indispensable motor for any company's profitability. In today's work environment, efficient leadership not only includes a superior's ability to build trustful and resilient relationships and to maintain them even under difficult circumstances. It particularly also requires someone with a stable personality, someone who knows his strengths and weaknesses and is therefore able to treat others in an authentic, composed and appreciative manner.

Research[34], however, has shown that a significant majority of executives are dissatisfied with the level of training and development when it comes to leadership competencies within their companies. According to the people who were interviewed, short-term success takes top priority and hinders the sustainable and systematic development of an effective leadership culture. In their own opinion, executives are currently limited in their ability to provide good leadership. They also wish they had significantly more support regarding the development of their leadership skills.

BREAKTHROUGH IN LEADERSHIP
///

On Amazon, you can find far more than a hundred thousand results for the term "leadership". Apparently, many experts have something to say on the topic, have an important opinion or know how it is done. At the same time, the hunger for answers in this field seems to be just as insatiable as unsatisfied. Many approaches are of an academic nature and explain leadership with the help of theories, methods and techniques which you only have to use and put into action in order to successfully lead people. This approach can work, but it often falls short. What is more, so far, most of these efforts, methods and techniques aimed to "increase employee motivation" do not deliver what they promise.

> ## "Leadership is the art of getting someone else to do something you want done because he wants to do it."
> DWIGHT D. EISENHOWER[35]

With the term "leadership" we describe the human oriented aspect of leadership, while the term "management" refers to the task related aspect of leadership. If we assume that leadership means exerting social influence and mobilization, then this poses the question: Is every manager automatically a leader as well? And does a leader necessarily have to be a manager? Both questions can safely be answered with a "no". Someone can be a leader, independent of his role or of what his business card says. This is true simply because the person has an impact, for example on a project team or when collaborating with others. This kind of "leading without power" will continue to gain greater and greater importance when strictly hierarchical organizations make room for increasingly network-like led organizations.

Natural authority shaped by high personal and interpersonal competence therefore becomes a crucial success factor when it comes to efficient leadership – independent of the job title. Then, people will do the things that are expected from them because they want to do them. Moreover, employees need to feel a sense of purpose because people only sincerely join in the game when they are able to recognize the purpose of the game, when they agree with the rules and, ideally, have the opportunity to actively influence the course of the game.

What Is Your Understanding Of Human Nature?

Another crucial factor for how you promote your understanding of leadership is the underlying understanding of human nature you have in your role as a leader. What do you think about people in general? What are your core beliefs when it comes to your employees? In his book The *Human Side of Enterprise* which was published in 1960, Douglas McGregor[36] describes two different views of human beings that shape the work of executives: The X- and the Y-Theory. Even though they are more than fifty years old, McGregor's management ideas still have great weight in this field and serve as the foundation for many other papers.

Executives with the X-Theory understanding of human nature assume that people are born with an aversion for work, that they are leisure time oriented and that they would rather do anything else than work. This makes external control and sanctions a requirement. People shy away from responsibility, they have no or little ambition and strive for security. Therefore, people have to receive external motivation and sanctions, and they have to be supervised.

On the other hand, there is the Y-Theory which describes an understanding of human nature that assumes that people experience work as a source of happiness and that they have a sense of responsibility, finding joy in performing and creativity – if you only let them. This promotes self-control and independent initiative as well as self-responsible and self-organized work. Human beings are able to motivate and supervise themselves – all they need is a framework for action and some instructions.

In both understandings, there is a verifiable momentum: In the case of the X-Theory, a downward spiral is created, a vicious cycle. When you assume that employees are unwilling to work and reluctant to assume responsibility, as their superior, you will issue strict rules and control. This will lead to employees being even more unwilling to work and reluctant to assume responsibility because they feel instrumentalized and have no leeway for shaping their environment. This in turn confirms your position and understanding of human nature from a supervisor's position – and you will continue to believe in your concept and style of leadership.

The same is true for the more positive understanding of human nature, the Y-Theory: Here, research has shown a reinforcing effect. When you assume that people have an innate drive to perform and are self-organized as well as responsible, you will encourage them to shape their environment and allow them to do things differently from how you would do them. You will exercise control only when it is necessary, even relying on self-control or peer-to-peer control where you deem it sufficient. This kind of leadership style will lead to your employees enjoying their work, exploiting their leeway, being self-organized as well as responsible and being committed and engaged in acting for the customer's and the company's benefit.

In an article titled "The Value of Happiness" that was published in the Harvard Business Review in 2012, the two authors Christine Porath[37] and Gretchen Spreitzer[38] describe how executives and organizations can support their employees in bringing a higher level of commitment to life. According to their findings, employees on any hierarchical level are particularly more engaged when they are able to make decisions on their own or at least influence those decisions that directly impact their work.

The airline industry offers a prime example of how this can work: Alaska Airlines managed to achieve a turnaround by conducting a cultural change which focused on providing maximum decision-making power to the front. Employees were invited to share their ideas of how service quality could be improved. They were asked to set aside their previous assessment of "good" service and instead, generate new ideas to take the service quality from "good" to a whole new level of "great". By doing so, individual customer needs could be fulfilled in a quick, independent and self-organized manner, without jeopardizing or affecting the flights' punctuality.

Another example of maximum freedom of action, self-organization and self-responsibility is found in the Swiss company Haufe Umantis, which is located in Appenzell and offers talent management solutions. Here, an employee-centered corporate culture actually has true meaning: In November of 2013, all executives subjected themselves to their 120 employees' vote. 25 candidates, consisting of CEO, COO as well as leaders and managers of ten teams were available for 21 positions. Eleven supervisors were confirmed in their position, seven employees were promoted into executive positions, three positions were filled with external candidates and one executive was removed from office. What do you think would happen in your company if the executives had to be elected by the employees?

Executives may have the power, but usually, the employees have the information. It is not a matter of conveying as much information as possible to higher levels, it is all about conveying as much power as possible to lower hierarchical levels. The English term used for this approach is »empowerment«. Or, as Steve Jobs put it: "It doesn't make sense to hire smart people and then tell them what to do." Self-organization and ownership can be achieved.

You Are Always A Role Model.

Leading means exerting influence. According to Nobel Prize winner Albert Schweitzer, serving as a role model is not only the best way to exert influence, it is the only way. But, as an executive, could you also not be a role model? The answer is no. Just like Paul Watzlawick explains in his well-known principle of communication: "You cannot *not* communicate", the same is true for leading people: "You cannot *not* serve as a role model."

The one who leads always sets an example. A good one or a bad one. Whether you are aware of this fact when operating in your role or not is irrelevant. You are under constant observation and people follow your example – and, by the way, this is even more true for what you do than what you say. This means it is wise to reflect upon your behavior as a leader, make yourself fully aware of it and carefully examine it regarding the question of whether it reflects the behavior you expect from your employees. Good leadership starts with good self-control and self-regulation. Or could you picture a really good executive who expects punctuality from her employees while always showing up late and regularly overrunning meetings?

It naturally makes sense to focus on displaying positive aspects to serve as a good example. For instance, a desire for positive change could be: "We need to start listening more carefully." In any change process, it has been proven to be more effective and sustainable to focus on creating something new instead of focusing on getting rid of the old. As an executive, it is well worth thinking about what you do as a leader which you should stop doing because it tends to demotivate your employees. In order to attain the defined goal of listening more carefully, this could mean you should stop playing with your smartphone while others are speaking. This is obviously not only true for your own behavior, but also for what you as an executive are willing to tolerate in others: "You get what you are willing to tolerate" is how one of my American colleagues aptly put it. Part of your role as an executive is to unmistakably demonstrate and be very clear about what kind of behavior you will not tolerate in others and to strictly stop, prevent or inhibit it accordingly.

> **"Half of all executives I have met don't need to learn what to do. They need to learn what to stop doing."**
> PETER DRUCKER[39]

Another important aspect in this context is the so-called resonance principle: If someone plays a violin in a room and a second violin is on a table in the same room, the second violin's strings and resonance body start vibrating in the same frequency as the violin that is being played. Resonance creates harmony.

The same is true for the correlation between the mood of an executive and the emotions of the people in his or her environment. The reason for this lies in the so-called "open loop" nature of the limbic system, the emotional center of our brain. A closed loop system is able to regulate itself while an open loop system depends on external factors to regulate itself. In other words: We rely on the contact to other people to regulate our various moods. For instance, based on this phenomenon, a mother is able to comfort her crying child.

This applies to the work environment as well – on a management team in the boardroom or in the manufacturing department. People are definitely affected by other people's moods. When it comes to the moods of higher-ranking employees, their moods are perceived even more quickly and intensely because more attention is focused on them by their employees. Even when the boss is not physically present and spends most of his time in his office, his attitude and moods still have an effect that cascades down through the business to his subordinates like a Domino game.

This is the reason why self-competence is of such great importance for executives. A self-competent superior is able to recognize his own moods and his emotional state based on his self-consciousness. He is able to exert positive influence on his emotions and mood through effective self-management, he recognizes the effect he has on others based on his empathetic skills and his social awareness and he is capable of steering his own behavior in such a manner that the mood of others is positively influenced through conscious relationship management. Self-competence is the spark that significantly impacts an organization's performance – and which leads to fireworks of success or scorched earth.

Relaxed Control With A Positive Focus

Effective leaders can be recognized by their relaxed control, among other things - independent of how high the waves might be raging at the time. An executive who manages to remain calm and in control despite - and particularly under - challenging conditions and when faced with a high level of negativity, creates and provides a sense of security, trust and orientation. When unpopular decisions have to be communicated, difficult talks have to take place, and insecurity as well as uncertainty impact the employees' commitment, this kind of leadership literally becomes a lighthouse, a tower of strength. In these situations, the executive serves as an example and as a role model for the employees - just by his or her presence and behavior alone.

Of course, the question of where an executive places the focus of attention plays a vital role. Due to the human negative bias, many executives mainly operate in the mode of problem solving. They catch employees making mistakes and give them negative and often unqualified feedback. By doing so, they do not necessarily create a beneficial climate. Instead, they create a climate in which the employees only have one goal: To survive, without taking a beating or being reprimanded. Accordingly, team members and the team as a group will tend to cover up mistakes, watch out for each other, hold back information and keep ideas to themselves while acting in and defending their best interests.

If employees are constantly in fight or flight mode due to their supervisor's problem focus, and therefore under constant stress, the brain puts them in survival mode. This means that every time they experience an ever so subtle form of rejection, their brain automatically reacts as though they were in a dangerous situation and goes into "red alert" mode. This is particularly true when they are treated in a disrespectful or disdainful manner, when they are subjected to unqualified criticism – especially if this takes place in front of other people. It is also the case when they are told what to do even if they know exactly what needs to be done or when they are not authorized to make a decision they feel they should be able to make themselves.

Taking on a positive focus is about directing your attention away from only looking at problems, mistakes etc. and instead focusing on growth, solutions and opportunities. Imagine the dynamics that are created when you put the focus of your leadership on opportunities: By discussing solutions after the occurrence of an error and not concentrating on finding out who is to blame. With this approach, you build a climate of growth, development, learning and advancement. This, in turn, will lead to your employees tending to learn from their mistakes, exchange ideas, develop creative approaches and supporting each other.

Imagine this approach would allow for commitment and passion to blossom during work hours and during leisure time. This would create amazing opportunities. However, you will only be able to direct the attention of your team towards opportunities and solutions if you are in a position to steer your own focus in the same direction.

Effective leaders have a primarily positive attitude. However, recognizing and addressing negative aspects plays a role that is just as important. Obviously, as an executive, you will not be able to avoid communicating the occasional changes that result in hurt, disappointment or worry for your employees. You have to be aware of the fact that in such a situation, the entire team and each individual may have to go through the valley of tears. It is not about putting up a brave front and shutting out all of the emotions. That would be cruel because we are emotional beings with emotional responses. If, for example, you have to tell an employee that he will be pulled from a project because his performance and level of commitment falls short of your expectations, then be aware that this message can push this employee into the valley of tears: His initial reaction might be to show resistance, which will then turn into anger, sadness and disappointment, followed by insecurity and concerns: "What does being pulled from this project mean for the future of my career in this company? What kind of impression does that leave in my resume?" It is possible for the employee to go through these stages in the course of the conversation you have with him – but it is also possible that this process will take several days or weeks.

Think about how you can adequately adjust your leadership style: While the other person is in the first stages of the valley of tears curve, it does not make much sense to explain to him the factual and rational arguments that led to the decision. You would not meet the employee where he is at if you took this approach. Even worse: He might be in an emotional state that does not even allow him to perceive factual and rational arguments. From a biological perspective, there is nobody there who could really listen to you in that situation.

What it actually takes instead is your presence, your empathy, for you to simply be there and your ability to maintain the relationship and contact with your employee, metaphorically speaking holding his hand in order to keep the relationship. It is all about supporting the employee and helping him get through the valley of tears – as quickly and efficiently as possible, without wanting to expedite the process. Be understanding and provide security and orientation where you can. It is important to be clear in your statements, be appreciative, empathetic and relationship oriented in the way you interact with your employee. Help him realign his focus, accept the situation and direct his attention towards the future and new opportunities as well as potential next steps that can be taken according to the new situation.

This applies to all kinds of situations in daily management routines. It does not have to be the message that someone is being let go. Even changes of less magnitude which still have negative consequences for employees and teams can lead to these processes and a journey through the valley of tears.

Take Off The Mask

A myth that is widespread among managers is that a superior must be able to do everything and know everything, and his leadership success is primarily based on technical competence. Therefore, for many people machismo and toughness are desirable, while sensitivity and vulnerability are seen as weaknesses. The decisive success factor in human leadership, however, lies in the ability to establish, build and maintain relationships even under difficult conditions. This ability has a lot to do with authenticity.

There are two main aspects to being authentic: Genuineness and vulnerability. Genuineness means showing your true self courageously, to be seen for who you are, even if this makes you feel uncomfortable. It means letting go of what you think you have to be, taking off the mask and armor and becoming visible as the person you really are, with your strengths and limitations. Vulnerability describes the willingness to admit that you don't have and don't have to have the solution to all problems. That you don't have all the knowledge needed in a particular situation. That you may even have made a mistake.

This latter aspect in particular seems to be difficult for many - and especially male - leaders, as making mistakes is often seen as a sign of weakness that must be avoided at all costs. However, this fear is in clear contrast to the actual effect such behavior usually has on employees. Experience shows that by acting this way, the leader is perceived as human and that acceptance, credibility and respect on the part of the team increase rather than decrease. In fact, we are most attracted by people we consider authentic, genuine and down-to-earth.

A leader who does not lead authentically does not dare to lower the protective armor under any circumstances – in case someone wants to "stab him in the back". By exemplifying this, the leader creates a climate in which only perfection is allowed - a climate in which macho behavior, false heroism and the pretense of strength are the order of the day. In this kind of setting, employees will tend to cover up mistakes and hide in order to get away with as little harm as possible. They will not dare to ask for help - even if they need it. And basically, the team members and the team as a whole will show less commitment.

On the other hand, an authentic leader has the courage to be himself in order to create an atmosphere and culture in which individual strengths are used effectively. Encouraged in this way, team members tend to develop their strengths, ask for help, support each other and feel connected, because through openness and authenticity relationships can be built faster and maintained longer. As a general rule, such a team shows a significantly higher level of commitment.

Place Your Trust In Your Employees

In leadership, trust is the connecting element based on which maximum performance is possible. Just like our emotional bank account, which is charged by some people and depleted out by others, the same goes for trust: In principle, we all have a trust account. Some people deposit, others withdraw. So first build trust within the company.

"If you want eggs, take care of the hen."
KAZUO INAMORI[40]

In the words of Richard Branson[41]: " Clients do not come first. Employees come first. If you take care of your employees, they will take care of the clients". A well-known example is Continental Airlines, a company that suffered from major trust problems in the 1980s and 1990s - until CEO Gordon Bethune took over. Until then, Continental's ranking was poor: Last place in punctuality and customer satisfaction as well as an unbelievably high staff turnover. One of Bethune's first measures was to introduce an open-door policy: No more locked doors on the executive floor at the headquarters. He made himself and his management team tangible and accessible to the employees, often worked in their presence and sometimes even helped with baggage handling. In doing so, he shaped a strongly team-oriented culture.

Building trust usually takes longer than breaking it. It comes naturally when we have repeated positive experiences with someone - experiences that show us that this person is trustworthy. But do we have that time in business? Of course, we don't. Therefore, trust is first and foremost a choice in the business world - and not the result of confidence-building experience. First of all, invest your trust in your employees, pay into the trust account, lay the foundation for valuable cooperation and act accordingly in your leadership. After all, how absurd would it be to look for qualified workers in the labor market, to choose them in the recruitment process - and then not trust them? Build trust by practicing trust. Trust is a decision.

Make Your Garden Bloom

When we look at leadership in the corporate world today, we find a large number of different styles. There are certainly successful organizations in which a very direct and controlling style still prevails, which can be described as "Command & Control". This very authoritarian style of leadership has its roots in the industrial age and is increasingly perceived as outdated in the working world of the 21st century. Nevertheless, this understanding of leadership works to some extent and I am not saying that it is wrong. Many organizations managed this way are extremely profitable and generate high shareholder value. One might well wonder, however, whether this is the only criterion for success and what price is paid for it. The consequences of such a leadership style often include high staff turnover and low employee engagement and loyalty. However, these are only of relative importance for the company as long as new applicants are queuing up.

There are, of course, situations in which a very directive form of leadership is necessary. This includes any crisis situations or other circumstances in which rapid and decisive action is required, i.e. in emergencies. If a Maître de Cabine and his crew experience an emergency, for example an aborted take-off due to fire in an engine, this is something that cannot be treated in a participative or collaborative management style. Here, a very direct leadership style is to be applied: Clear instructions, clear commands.

In such situations the maintenance of the relationship naturally fades into the background and things can get rough and loud. After such missions, however, a debriefing is held, an exchange to ensure that the relationships are intact and that anyone who has been involved can leave the situation in a state of emotional stability. That was the case in aviation, in my assignments with CareLink and that is the case with all blue light organizations (emergency services) after they complete a mission. Unfortunately, however, many leaders have a constantly directive style - regardless of the situation and also during normal operation. With the corresponding effect on relationships.

At the other end of the spectrum, there is an increasing number of managers and entrepreneurs who live an understanding of leadership based on partnership: They do this by creating a framework in which every employee and the team as a whole can perform at their best. This type of leadership is primarily about the employees, not about their superiors. Or as Warren Bennis, the recently deceased author and leadership pioneer aptly said: "Good managers give their employees the feeling that they are at the center of things, not on the periphery." From this point of view, management definitely takes on a service character with the aim of creating optimal conditions so that every employee in the team can flourish in the best possible way, utilize his or her potential and therefore make a significant contribution to the success of the company.

Let us elaborate for a moment on the term "blooming" and the comparison with the plant in the "Self-Exploration" section: In principle, this understanding of leadership makes you a gardener. Your company is a diverse garden, where different plants can be found: Your employees. Each of these plants only needs optimal conditions to bloom and to become what it is: An oak, a fir, an orchid. None of these plants will grow faster if you pull on them. None of them will become something they're not. And it is not enough to pull the weeds, to simply dust the leaves from time to time and spray them with a little water if the other conditions are not right.

The right soil, enough light, the right temperature and water are the main components they need to grow. In a figurative sense, the ground stands for the company and the meaningfulness it represents for the employee. The light stands for the management's focus on growth and opportunities. Have you ever planted a plant seed in your garden and watched it fight its way up through the earth and then immediately turn to the sun? People behave very similarly. We are attracted to people who radiate a positive energy and avoid contact with those who radiate negativity. The temperature stands for the right climate of appreciation and trust that your employees experience every day. And the water corresponds to the regular positive feedback on their performance which they receive from their superiors.

Strong growth also requires a certain type of fertilizer. This fertilizer is called "enthusiasm". If you manage to plant the plants in the right place in your company and then fertilize them with enthusiasm, then you create the best conditions for your employees to grow and develop into what they can be. This can be achieved, for example, by regularly creating space and opportunities for new experiences that ideally lie outside the comfort zone in order to grow. Of course, this also means that you have to endure experiencing your employees outside their comfort zone - and do not want to "save" them immediately if the situation becomes unpleasant for them - knowing that something very important is happening, namely a process of learning, development and growth.

Looking at it from this point of view, there are basically no low performers, only the right people in the wrong place. Success arises, among other things, when a person's profile and potential match the requirements of a role, its tasks and responsibilities in the best possible way. I have already seen many examples of companies who wanted to let employees go and decided to look for a different position internally at first, so that all the know-how and experience would stay within the company. In many cases it turned out that the person flourished in the new role within a very short time and became extremely successful in it.

Lead Individually And According To The Situation

It is therefore not a question of choosing one leadership style as a manager and then applying it to all employees according to the scattergun principle, but of applying the most effective leadership style for each employee. A basic attitude of partnership in leadership is therefore particularly effective when it is combined with a situational leadership approach. This concept, originally developed by Paul Hersey[42] and later further developed by Ken Blanchard[43], comprises four main leadership styles, each of which corresponds to one of four employee development stages, the so-called maturity level. This is defined by the competence of the employee and by his or her engagement and is often referred to as the "Skill/Will Matrix". Here are the four leadership styles with the corresponding degree of maturity of the employee:

Directive

The leader gives precise instructions and supervises the implementation conscientiously. This style is recommended for employees at maturity level 1, which is determined by (still) low competence and high commitment. Typically, these are employees who are new to the company or new to another function after an internal change. A new employee needs guidance and directive leadership. The "what" and "how" is specified by the superior.

Training
The leader continues to conscientiously monitor and direct the execution of the task, but discusses her decisions with the employees, asks them for suggestions and supports their progress. This style corresponds to maturity level 2, where we speak of some competence and high engagement. Regarding the competence, there is still room for development and the level of engagement is high.

Supporting
The leader promotes and supports the employees in carrying out the task and shares responsibility for the decisions to be made together with them. Maturity level 3 is characterized by high competence and fluctuating commitment. Typically, these are long-standing employees who know a lot and are highly competent, but whose engagement is unstable.

Delegating
The leader transfers the responsibility for the decision-making and problem-solving to the employee. Maturity level 4 means high competence and high engagement. Here we usually find future leaders, self-starters, employees who are best given maximum freedom of action, tasks and responsibility completely delegated as a package and who are included in decision-making or even goal setting. In short: Create optimal conditions and then get out of the way.

At one end of the spectrum, the directive leadership style, you guide the employees in a very directive manner with clear instructions for action and clearly define both the goal and the path to achieving it. In this tight leadership, which can best be compared to the aforementioned "Command & Control" style, it is crucial that it is performed with a sufficiently strong relationship orientation. This is why I prefer calling it "Command & Care". If you tell your employee what and how to do something with a benevolent and appreciative attitude, then he will not perceive it as an order, but as what it is: Simply a clear instruction.

At the other end of the spectrum, the delegating leadership style, you delegate and agree on the goal together with the employee. Ideally, the employee will make a target proposal for you, which you discuss and agree upon. In this way, the employee decides for himself how to achieve his goals: Independently, self-organized, self-determined - and therefore proud, satisfied and committed.

This results in a simple and variable system where you determine which leadership style suits each employee in your team and what he or she needs to deliver the best possible performance. It also becomes clear what the consequences of an incorrectly chosen leadership style can be: If you lead an employee with a high degree of maturity in a very directive way, she will perceive you as a micro-manager and you will not only be very ineffective, but in the worst case even counterproductive. The employee does not feel that her competence is being recognized and her engagement will inevitably decline. On the other hand, if you give an employee with a low degree of maturity a very high degree of freedom of action, it is possible that you are completely overwhelming him, giving him too little orientation and thus too little security and he ultimately feels lost. This is also ineffective and can lead to demotivation, too.

Stay In Touch: Feedback and Feedforward

What thoughts come to your mind spontaneously when you read or hear the term "feedback"? What is your spontaneous inner reaction when the boss comes to you and says: "May I give you some feedback?" Like many people, you probably flinch inwardly, because you don't necessarily expect a beautiful bouquet of flowers, but rather the proverbial hammer. Unfortunately, many people have already internalized the term "feedback" as an emotive word.

There are two main reasons for this: The first is that most superiors have the above-mentioned mindset with a problem-solving focus and therefore primarily notice mistakes, shortcomings and deficits – on which they give feedback. The second reason is that unqualified feedback is still given far too often: Superiors distribute all-round strikes, generalize, evaluate, judge and condemn. This is not very helpful.

But there is another way. We now know that companies, departments or divisions with an explicit feedback culture - a culture in which it is common practice to give each other constructive, positive, but also critical feedback in a brain-friendly way - generally have a better working atmosphere characterized by trust and mutual support. These companies also enjoy a higher level of employee engagement and are accordingly profitable. Feedback creates opportunities to learn and an energy that is crucial for a culture of blooming. The more immediate and direct the feedback, the more effective it will be. It is also the most effective tool for reducing blind spots.

So how do you provide qualified feedback? Well, first of all there is a difference between praise and feedback: Praise is always positive, feedback can - at least as it is commonly understood - also be "negative". The main difference between praise and feedback is that praise is a feedback on an emotional level: "Hey, that was really great, your presentation!" It's good, it's appreciated and we need it. It is important and right to give praise. Please do not lead according to the principle "Not scolding is praised enough" - your employees will thank you if you praise them again and again in a genuine, authentic and serious way. It helps them recharge their emotional batteries.

In contrast to praise, feedback is more specific. If your supervisor gives you praise for your presentation after the meeting, it makes you feel good - but does it tell you what you'll have to do next time to get praise again? No, it doesn't - because praise isn't specific enough. That's why feedback is about giving as precise and timely feedback as possible on observed behavior - and not just once a year in a performance meeting. It should be constructive, respectful and complete and not analytical, interpretive or judgmental. In general, the basic attitude should be that the feedback is a gift for the recipient, which he can accept without stress and without falling into a fight or flight reaction, even if it contains critical aspects. There are a few ground rules for doing that. If you comply with them, even critical feedback will be accepted more easily and even gratefully. To do this, consistently separate three things:

First: Your own perception
Describe the perceived situation in concrete terms. Refer only to the facts and the observed behavior and refrain from making any interpretations as to why someone behaved in a certain way, or generalizations.
An example: For reasons unknown to you, your employee did not show the same energy in the meeting this morning as usual. Unqualified feedback would be: "Listen, you were totally demotivated in the meeting this morning. You didn't look like being there at all!" This is firstly unspecific, secondly judgmental, thirdly an interpretation. A qualified feedback of observed behavior could instead sound like this: "At the meeting this morning you didn't even get involved in the discussion. I didn't see the same level of engagement in you as usual."

Secondly: The effect the observed behavior has on you
Describe the effects this behavior has on you. Here you can also incorporate your emotions, for example by saying: "I was a little disappointed that you didn't get involved today".

Thirdly: Wishes, expectations, recommendations
For example: "I would appreciate it if you could show more active engagement in the next meeting and contribute more to the discussion".

I also like to refer to the third step as "feedforward", a term that Marshall Goldsmith coined in this context. While feedback refers to the retrospective response to what has already been achieved, feedforward sheds light on the recommendations for more effectiveness in the future.

For example: Perhaps your employee has shown strengths in her presentation, while at the same time you still see potential for improvement. A combination of feedback and feedforward could then sound like this: "What I particularly liked today was how you chose a strong introduction in your presentation and immediately gained the full attention of your audience." So, this is a review with a positive focus. Instead of now giving "negative" feedback by continuing: "But what I didn't like was that you didn't get involved in the subsequent discussion," you focus on the future and make a recommendation. For if you say: "I liked this, but I did not like this and that", what remains of it above all? The negative, of course. In addition, you also said "but". Basically, you could have omitted everything before the comma.

Instead, you could say: "What I really liked about your presentation today was the strong start: You managed to keep the audience's attention right from the start. To be even more effective in the future, I recommend that you take a short break after important statements. That way you give more weight to the statement. Try to pay more attention to this in the future. " Hear the difference? The focus is first on the strengths and then on recommendations for the future. Because in the future I can change something - and if I get valuable information about it, all the better.

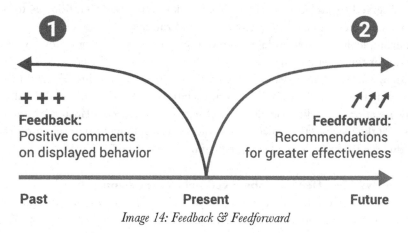

Image 14: Feedback & Feedforward

You've probably already noticed: The feedforward is where the criticism is wrapped-up. What you may have given as critical or negative feedback so far, you continue to give - only in different packaging! And in such a way that it is much easier and more pleasant for the recipient to accept than "What I liked ... **but** what I didn't like ...".

So: Become a feedback and feedforward professional! Use the way our perception works and give feedback and feedforward, so that you motivate your employees instead of demotivating them and create a corresponding climate of trust, mutual support and engagement in your company by reinforcing what's working well and fostering a culture of growth and development.

//

STOPOVER - LEADERSHIP

Use your own words to summarize what you have learned for yourself in this last chapter and what kind of information you consider to be the most important or helpful for you.

_____

_____

_____

_____

_____

_____

_____

_____

Think about the findings you would like to transfer to your professional or personal life. What kind of intentions have already begun to take root and where do you see opportunities to put them into practice?
elpful for you.

_____

_____

_____

_____

_____

_____

_____

_____

//

DESTINATION TEAMWORK

//

Image 15: Destination Teamwork

ABOVE THE CLOUDS

///

I was up early that September morning because I was scheduled to work on a flight to Chicago. I had breakfast in peace, packed my things and got in my car, a small VW Polo. As soon as I left, I turned on the radio, as usual, and drove towards the airport. As I was accelerating and getting onto the motorway, the morning news was just starting. I will never forget the speaker's words: "Last night, a Swissair plane crashed near Halifax off Canada's east coast. The flight took off from New York last night and should have arrived in Geneva this morning. Almost two hours after take-off from New York's John F. Kennedy airport, the plane disappeared from the radar screens with 229 people on board."

I was sitting in the car with my mouth open, thinking, "This can't be true! At the same time, I knew it had to be: One of our MD-11 machines with the enrollment HB-IWF had crashed into the Atlantic near the Canadian coastal town of Halifax, about eight kilometers from the small fishing village of Peggy's Cove.

A thousand thoughts were racing through my mind as I was driving to the airport, as if on autopilot. Which of my colleagues had been on board? Feeling completely dazed, I arrived. As I walked through the long tunnel from the parking garage to the OPS, I met a colleague. "Have you heard?" he asked. I nodded, but I didn't get a word out. When we arrived at the other end of the corridor, the atmosphere was filled with disbelief, dismay, grief and pain which you could physically feel. Everywhere you saw uniformed pilots and flight attendants talking to each other, some hugging each other, others crying. It seemed like a dream, surreal and almost creepy.

Soon the names of the crew members were known: I had worked with more than half of them once or several times. Memories came alive with shared experiences and conversations. It was a heartbreaking loss to our big family. I have never forgotten what I experienced in the days, weeks and months that followed the Halifax crash. These were moving, profound moments, moments of indescribable compassion, humanity and cohesion that shaped everything. I became even more aware that we really were like one big family and stuck together even in those dark hours.

At the OPS-Center in Zurich, a memorial was soon erected where colleagues could put flowers, commemorative cards and mourning cards, where candles were lit and where the photos of our colleagues who had died in the crash were displayed.

If you consider what constitutes a team, boarding an aircraft and taking off for a destination together is just that. A team primarily differs from a group in that it has a common goal and a common meaningful purpose it pursues. This physical boarding-a-plane and flying-to-the-final-destination is a strong impetus for teamwork. In addition, a good team is characterized by mutual trust, which is really important for a flight crew, because there are interdependencies, especially in the area of safety.

Never again did I experience the same spirit and culture of togetherness in a company as I did at Swissair. The sense of purpose was a great motivator, especially for flying personnel. I didn't know anyone who didn't proudly wear the uniform of this company and went to work full of joy. Nobody did this because of the money - that would have been ridiculous, given the initial wages. Something else drove us: The need to contribute to being one of the best airlines in the world, to make a significant contribution to the overall experience of our passengers and therefore creating an unforgettable experience for other people.

This profession attracts a certain kind of person: People with a high degree of relationship orientation, who by nature tend to be more outgoing, customer-centered and altruistic, in contrast to a high degree of factual or task orientation. This high relationship orientation was not only evident in customer contact, but also in the mutual support within the team: I was always amazed at how we crew members supported each other, looked after each other and made sure that we were doing well. This, of course, was strongly influenced by what the Maître de Cabine exemplified: Was he someone who just looked after himself first, was he the first to sit down after the meal service to eat something himself - or was he someone who first ensured that everyone else was provided for and only sat down to eat something himself when everything and everyone else was taken care of?

The teamwork of the flying personnel was something that naturally took place at different levels: Firstly, the cooperation between the individual crew members and between the first class, business class and economy class compartments. Then the teamwork between the cabin crew and the cockpit crew and between the cabin crew and the ground crew. As Maître de Cabine, I had an interface function between the three areas of cockpit, ground and cabin, especially shortly before take-off.

In fact, there were many interfaces in the cooperation between the cockpit and the cabin crew and the quality of communication was crucial. The two teams had different load curves: While it was high for both teams during the flight preparations on board, the load curves during the flight were different: For the cockpit crew it was very high during the take-off and climb phases and then decreased again during cruising flight. From "top of descent" it rose again and remained high until after landing. In the final approach, the so-called "silent-cockpit-rule[44]" applied, because this was the phase with the highest workload for the pilots.

In the cabin, the load curve was exactly the opposite: During take-off and landing - apart from a high level of alertness and concentration - little direct work load, but rather an alert "standby mode". However, immediately after take-off, as soon as the cruising altitude was reached, the load curve rose abruptly. For short-haul flights it usually remained high until the end, for long-haul flights it decreased after the first meal service and increased again before landing with the second meal service or landing preparations. Mutual knowledge of these different load curves, the resulting understanding of the requirements and the consistent respect for each of those duties was decisive for smooth operations.

The strong team cooperation across all areas changed the moment Swissair became the holding company SAirGroup and the various parts of the airline were split into separate companies. This demarcation between the individual areas had a noticeable effect on the quality of collaboration. What used to operate under one brand was now independent businesses that had to be profitable on their own. This was of a different quality, especially when it came to working with ground staff: They notably started to look after themselves more and the cross-functional team cooperation was affected as a result. In my opinion, this meant that a part of the Swissair spirit was lost and "silo thinking" increased.

CHALLENGES IN TEAMWORK
//

There are many challenges in the cooperation of employees. Diversity alone, resulting from differences in personality, value orientation, views, beliefs and interests, and cultural differences, provides fertile ground for friction, disagreement and conflict. These challenges can arise on two levels:

// Within a team
// Between different teams

Within teams, I often experience that an insufficient understanding of roles, inconsistent distribution of tasks and a lack of clarity regarding responsibilities leads to major frictional losses. In addition, there are often incentive systems in place that promote competitive thinking and actual competition instead of encouraging cooperation and an orientation towards a common goal, while executives and managers wonder why a sincere team spirit does not develop.

Cooperation in many teams is affected by smoldering or more or less open conflicts. Sometimes this even goes so far that the real reason for existing tensions, rejections and conflicts is no longer really clear to those involved, but only the fixed picture of the other and the feelings associated with it remain - which still permanently hinder cooperation. In the worst case, employees stop talking to each other and avoid each other as best they can. We are talking about a cold conflict that usually can no longer be resolved without external support.

Ideally, this support can be provided by the direct superior. But even here, there are many cases in which the superiors themselves are under great pressure for reasons already mentioned. They may also lack methodological competence and have underdeveloped personal and interpersonal competencies and are therefore hopelessly overwhelmed by the situation. Depending on the personality, the supervisor then intervenes and "solves" the situation by using pressure and force - for example by dismissing one or both employees. Or the supervisor closes his eyes to the situation, buries his head in the sand and hopes that the issue will resolve itself - which of course is noticed by all employees in the team and is damaging for the acceptance and credibility of the manager.

Another challenge for effective collaboration of teams within companies is that this is not exemplified by the managers: Members of the executive management board often do not truly collaborate as a team in management bodies, management teams, supervisory boards and boards of directors. This sends signals to the company accordingly, because they are not perceived as a team. Background are often power struggles, differing views on strategic orientation and implementation, latent conflicts at the relationship level or in the worst case even openly fought out conflicts that are not tackled and solved and thus exert a strong influence on the entire organization. In many companies there are rivalries, trench warfare and competitive thinking between the departments - the so-called "silo thinking", which, in Switzerland, is also called "garden thinking" which sounds somewhat better, but is exactly the same.

As a result of this, members of the management team identify primarily with their own organizational units, defend their interests and shield them from the outside world like silos. The hierarchical levels below observe and adopt that which is exemplified to them from "above". This behavior, which is not very helpful for collaboration within teams and between teams in different areas, cascades into the organization, is transferred to the lower hierarchy levels and strengthens silo thinking within the company.

There are many reasons for this. In my work as a coach, for example, I often experience that the necessary leadership skills are more often present at the middle management level, rather than at the higher executive levels: Employees work together in a relationship-building, constructive and solution-focused manner and try to set an example, which has a positive effect. On the upper floors, however, what the middle management level has demonstrated in terms of change and positive management behavior is often poorly demonstrated, if at all. One reason for this is that, due to the incentives offered by higher management positions - including an increase in power - we see predominantly male and rather dominant personalities with a high task orientation in such positions who may not necessarily have the relationship orientation and the desire to lead people. Due to a lack of awareness of the problem, there is often a lack of openness and willingness to pay the required attention to these aspects or even to develop the corresponding competencies.

This is why there is often an imbalance in the upper management levels in favor of intellectual intelligence (IQ), rationality, technical and professional competence, factually logical decision-making, assertiveness etc., at the expense of empathy in dealing with employees, customers, suppliers and other people - and thus at the expense of interpersonal competence and emotional intelligence.

One of the keys to eliminating this silo thinking is that top-level managers and executives focus on working together as a management team, i.e. pushing team building and development and focusing on cross-divisional collaboration. In this way, leaders exemplify what they want to see in the organization: Cross-departmental, customer-oriented behavior to the benefit of the entire organization.

BREAKTHROUGH IN TEAMWORK
//

Normally everyone wants to work in a good team. If things don't work properly, it's often the fault of the other members - that's a natural attitude. Conflicts are unpleasant, but normal. For a team to become and remain effective, regular team maintenance is necessary. This can be compared with the engine of a car: To ensure that it runs well for a long time and can achieve maximum performance, it must be serviced regularly. If maintenance is neglected, damage may not be detected in time and expand until the engine runs bumpy, stops or even causes irreparable damage. This is even more true for high performance engines such as the ones used in Formula 1 cars.

The same is true for a team. If you spend too much time not caring about the relationships and about what happens beneath the surface, you will not notice the early indicators soon enough or not at all. Then the situation can deteriorate noticeably within the team.

But what is a team anyway? The term originates from the English language and initially described a bullock cart. This makes sense: The oxen pull a cart together. So, it's about making a difference in and through cooperation. By definition, the team differs from the group: Employees who work together in the same room do not have to be a team for that reason alone. A team emerges when they work together on a topic in order to achieve a common goal. Everyone can work on a different aspect, but the goal is a common one. A team is a group of people with complementary skills who work together towards a common goal or vision. Team spirit also develops particularly strongly when the team even has a common problem to be solved which affects everyone. Because you can also say goodbye to a common goal - internally or even officially.

> **"A team is not a group of people who work together –**
> **a team is a group of people who trust each other."**
> SIMON SINEK[45]

When employees from different departments are put together to form a project team to pursue a common goal, it is important to note that each team member also pursues his or her own goals, which may have nothing to do with the project. If these cannot be brought into line with the project goal or even contradict it, it can become difficult - especially if the individual's own goals have a higher priority to them than the team goal, which is usually the case. Then it can feel like the handbrake is set, even though everyone is on the gas pedal and saying, "Yeah, we understand what it's all about and we're all fully motivated. " We are talking about a "conflict of goals" that can ultimately lead to a zero-sum game, because the commitment and intentions of the different goals point to different directions.

But why teamwork? We could simply say: "Let everyone work on their own topic, that way we have less points of contact and therefore fewer problems and conflicts". But working together as a team has its advantages: The team often knows more than the individual and the results are better. The team can compensate for extreme differences: If, for example, a woman joins a purely male team, the mood and interaction with each other usually changes. This is not only gender-specific, but generally applies to diversity in the team.

Furthermore, the team can provide support and human cohesion: We are social beings and by nature hard-wired to work together and support each other. And this support, this human cohesion is simply more likely to happen in a team.

The strength of a team does therefore not lie in its similarities, but above all in its differences. The similarities facilitate mutual access to each other and the creation and maintenance of relationships, but the true strength of a team - especially in the area of creativity and problem solving - lies in diversity.

Team Building Blocks

Five basic building blocks are needed for effective team cooperation. If we look at them against the background of the cabin crews at Swissair, it becomes clear why teamwork there worked so well:

Building block no. 1: Purpose

The purpose forms the basis of teamwork, results from the assignment and ensures that the whole team has a common understanding of the "why": What is our "raison d'être", our reason to exist, and where are we going together? At Swissair, the meaning and purpose no longer had to be clarified or specified - it was clear to all of us, because we worked day in day out in harmony with our sense of purpose and our values.

Building block no. 2: Goals

Goals set the direction and define a common vision and motivation from which individual performance targets can be derived. At Swissair, the goals were always clarified: Providing an exceptional customer experience while at the same time ensuring maximum passenger safety. There was no discussion about it.

Building block no. 3: Relationships

Good relationships are vital for the cooperation in the team. They must be marked by trust. Differences and similarities must be clarified. This is about mutual support and being there for each other. The relationships among cabin crew members were basically characterized by a high degree of relationship orientation, empathy, mutual support, perception and being in contact.
We had brought this being-connected with each other into our work from the very beginning.

Building block no. 4: Roles and tasks

Everyone has his or her place in the team, so the rules of the game for cooperation are defined and all the individual team members know their role in the team. The roles and tasks in the cabin were absolutely clear: Before and after working for Swissair, I never experienced another company or job where the roles and tasks were so clearly defined. Everyone knew what his task and responsibility was. There was a very high level of personal responsibility on the one hand and a sense of responsibility for the well-being of the entire team and the joint task on the other.

Building block no. 5: Processes

Defined processes and structures as well as common working methods have to be agreed upon and keep the whole operation together. At Swissair, processes were defined with different precision in both of the cabin crew's main areas of responsibility - passenger safety and customer service. With regard to passenger safety, there were clearly defined processes, so-called "procedures", which had to be adhered to one hundred percent exactly as they were defined. There were checklists, site plans of emergency equipment and procedures that had to be followed in different types of incidents such as smoke development or cabin fires. All this was very clearly defined. In the service area, the specifications were less clearly defined and allowed more leeway.

Psychological Safety

Technology giant Google hired a team of consultants to find out what it really needed to bring a productive, high-performance team together. The project, called "Aristotle", was rolled out over several years and included interviews with hundreds of employees and data analyses from over a hundred active teams within the group. The consultants were looking for a magic formula - the perfect mix of employees and personalities in terms of diversification - to form an outstanding team.

Google's data-driven approach ultimately revealed what executives had been suspecting for some time: The best teams respect each other's emotions and ensure that all employees are equally involved in communication and exchange. It has less to do with who is on the team than with how the team members interact with each other. This finding is consistent with Steven Covey's influential book *The Seven Habits of Highly Effective People*: Members of effective teams take the effort to truly understand each other, to be in contact with each other, to build relationships with each other, and to express themselves in such a way that they are understood.

Matt Sakaguchi, a manager at Google, wanted to immediately put the findings of the Aristotle project into practice. He invited his team members to an offsite and shared his cancer diagnosis with them. The initial reaction of his colleagues was silence, but then they all started telling their personal stories. At the heart of Sakaguchi's strategy and the findings of the Google study lies the concept of *psychological safety* - a model of team collaboration in which all members of a team agree that it is safe to share a variety of ideas and views without fear of being humiliated or exposed.

Amy C. Edmondson of Harvard Business School further examined the concept in a 1999 study and came to the conclusion that psychological safety can massively increase the performance of teams. Today, Google describes psychological safety as the most important factor in the formation of successful teams. In short: Respect each other and cultivate a respectful and friendly relationship with each other.

Phases Of Team Development

A team cannot just be put together and then be expected to perform optimally right from the start. That would be great, but in practice things usually works differently - with a few exceptions. An exception to this is the airline industry, where flight crews are reassembled for each flight and then have to perform well immediately. These teams are welded together in briefings and aligned to a common goal and common expectations. This requires a high level of professionalism, a high level of standardization and clarity with regard to the aforementioned team building blocks.

In development, a team goes through certain phases, which Bruce Tuckman described as *Forming, Storming, Norming* and *Performing*:

The forming or founding phase is the time in which the team is created or newly formed - for example, a project team. The tasks in this phase are to get to know and assess each other, to position oneself loosely and to find a common denominator. The goal is to establish sustainable contacts, but the climate could be rather subdued. In order to lead according to this phase, the leader must take on the role of captain and facilitator and lead in a tight, goal-oriented manner with a clear definition of the assignment and a clear framework, creating space and opportunities for social contacts and getting to know each other. This means clarity and orientation at the factual level and a high degree of relationship orientation, creating opportunities for establishing contacts and relationships.

The second team development phase is called storming or dispute phase. The tasks of the team in this phase are to recognize and clarify differences, to solve conflicts and to identify similarities. The climate can be stormy and conflict-prone. In this stage, phase-oriented leadership means that the leader slips into the role of a process facilitator, creates space for the handling and resolution of conflicts, ensures an open and trustworthy communication climate and contributes to the clarification of misunderstandings, uncertainties, fears and anxieties. Most importantly, the leadership is aware that the storming phase is a normal and natural team development phase, which does not necessarily mean that the engine is breaking down - but that it is part of the engine running-in process. The worst thing an executive can do in the storming phase is to keep the lid on the boiling pressure cooker to prevent conflict.

The norming phase is the standardization or contract phase. In this phase, the team's task is to take stock of the forming and storming phases, to commit itself and perhaps also to say goodbye to illusions to a certain extent. Perhaps it becomes clearer what is possible and what is not with this team. This phase therefore leads to clarification. The goal is a framework contract, a team contract - in the sense of an agreement with common rules for cooperation. The climate here is rather rational. In the norming phase, effective leadership means above all assuming the role of the coach - supporting, accompanying, enabling and guiding the drafting and negotiation of this team contract.

The fourth phase is the so-called performance or delivery phase. The tasks of the team are to check the agreed rules of cooperation from the team contract again and again for practical suitability, to adapt them if necessary and to provide optimal performance. You can immediately sense this when you join a team that is in the performing phase: Things run smoothly. There is an atmosphere of flow, high concentration, cooperation, commitment and also fun with very high performance at the same time. That's exactly what you want from a team. As the process clearly indicates, it is the final part of the four development phases which a team normally goes through. In the performing phase, the executive is in the role of the captain who comes on board when difficult circumstances arise. He guides the team through challenges, accompanies, supports, gives orientation and then leaves the boat again. In this phase, the leader ideally takes a back seat - "leading from behind" is the term - like the driver of a husky-drawn sled, who stands behind and lets the team (his dogs) perform in front.

This development process sounds fairly static with clear beginnings and endings. However, it is a very dynamic journey that can start all over again at any time. Assuming that a team is in the performing phase and there is a change in the system - for example, the superior changes, a member leaves, a new one joins or the team, the goal, the roles are changed by a reorganization - then the four-phase process starts all over again. This means that a forming phase is needed again, a repositioning. The process may be faster, but it is especially important as a leader to recognize that the team will pass through all the phases again.

It becomes clear that there are certain risks at each of these stages of the process. Especially in storming and norming the risk is high that the team gets stuck and does not make it to the next phase without support. These are big tasks for the leadership and therefore it is important for the superior to recognize these phases and to be aware again and again which leadership behavior is appropriate in these phases and what the team needs. In the sense of good self-management and well-developed self-confidence, the manager should sit down together with the team and say: "Where do we stand, where do we want to go and what do we need to get there? How can we support each other, how can leadership support you and what can everyone contribute as an individual?"

A fifth phase, which I call the "reforming phase" or "orientation phase", can consciously initiate this process: In contrast to the forming phase, reforming is deliberately initiated, for example for a joint assessment of the situation and reorientation. If the team as a whole has been in the comfort zone for a longer period of time, such a step can be very helpful. The aim is to appreciate the team's performance, to make people aware of what has been achieved, to put topics on the table where change is desired and to review the team's vision and, if necessary, to adapt it. Here it can also be helpful to enable new experiences which lie outside the comfort zone, in order to promote growth and an increase in the resilience of the team. In this way you give the team and its needs the necessary attention and perform what I referred to as "team maintenance" at the beginning of this section.

Tuckman himself also defined a fifth phase, which he referred to as "adjourning", meaning the dissolution of a team. So, this phase is about ending the cooperation after the task of the team has been fulfilled and the goal ideally reached and the team members turn to other tasks. From the organization's point of view, the most important thing here is to show recognition and appreciation for what has been achieved, especially if strong connections and relationships have been created through cooperation. The dissolution of the team can lead to a feeling of insecurity among individuals.

What Is The Team's Situation?

Often, we have a vague feeling for the situation in the team - tense, unstable, committed, sometimes like this, sometimes different - or the situation between teams of different departments. In order to create a little more tangibility here, a simple instrument is suitable for visualizing the situation: The "sociogram" developed by Jacob Levy Moreno[46].

To create a sociogram of your team, start by drawing a circle in the middle of a sheet of paper, in which you write "I". Around it you arrange the other members of your team and label them with their names or initials. Then you begin to record the quality of the relationships between individual team members, and between you and the team members, by making connections between the circles. Depending on whether it is a good, resilient relationship or a disturbed, charged relationship, for example, you can use red and green color - or you can draw charged relationships with a dashed line so that you can see right away what kind of relationship it is. This makes it very easy to see where strained relationships accumulate and where someone in the team has many positive relationships, which usually means that they radiate positive energy.

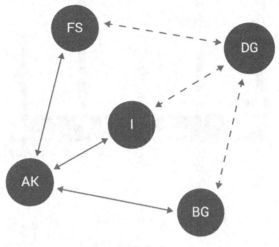

Image 16: Sociogram

With a certain probability, the sociogram does not contain any surprises since it only confirms what you already feel, but it presents this visually and thus makes it more tangible. You can also fill it out together with the team - not only if you have a leadership role: As an employee, you can also sit down with your colleagues and draw a sociogram. This can reveal different perceptions or even unity regarding the perception of the team.

And this brings me to the next model to illustrate the situation in the team: The so-called "force field analysis", which goes back to Kurt Lewin[47] and is about illustrating the driving and hindering factors in a situation or in a team. It can be represented in different ways: For example, draw a horizontal line as a zero line and draw arrows up or down at right angles to it for individual team members, depending on how much commitment and beneficial energy or how much braking power and obstructive energy someone is showing in a project, so you get a kind of energy balance. Perhaps this will help you to see why something is not moving forward with the desired speed and the desired commitment.

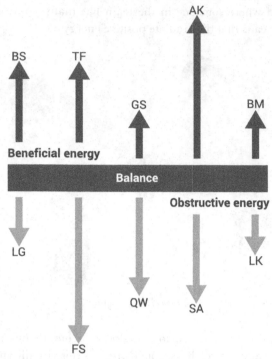

Image 17: Force field analysis

Both instruments are suitable for making things visible that you may be perceiving, but may not be able to describe so clearly. On the basis of a visualization, it is easier to talk to colleagues or your superiors about the situation. You can also combine the two approaches, for example by varying the size of the different circles in the sociogram, depending on the energy and commitment someone brings into the team - or does not.

Whenever possible, create opportunities for your team to meet and exchange informally and on a voluntary basis so that relationships can be established, built and maintained.

///

STOPOVER - TEAMWORK

Use your own words to summarize what you have learned for yourself in this last chapter and what kind of information you consider to be the most important or helpful for you.

_____

_____

_____

_____

_____

_____

_____

_____

_____

Think about the findings you would like to transfer to your professional or personal life. What kind of intentions have already begun to take root and where do you see opportunities to put them into practice?

_____

_____

_____

_____

_____

_____

_____

///

DESTINATION CUSTOMER CONTACT

//

Image 18: Destination Customer Contact

ABOVE THE CLOUDS

//

My roster showed a North Atlantic flight: Zurich – Chicago. On December 24, Christmas Eve. I didn't mind, at the time. I was even excited about spending Christmas abroad. Chicago certainly wasn't the worst place to be during that special season. My flight preparations included checking the weather forecast and it looked like I was going to be a truly white Christmas. So, I particularly looked forward to this flight and thought about what I could do to show my crew how much I appreciated their commitment and hard work and turn this flight into a unique experience for our passengers.

I came up with the idea of surprising our passengers with Christmas cookies. The day before the flight, I went to the store, bought some Christmas cookie dough, and brought it to the briefing I shared all necessary information with my crew, placed great value on a safety briefing as usual, worked through my check list.... And then shared that we would be doing something very special on this flight: Baking Christmas cookies. I passed around the packed dough rolls together with some cookie cutters in the shapes of stars, crescent moons etc. We were all joyfully giggling when we walked to the plane to start our flight preparations.

Following the meal service, we started baking the Christmas cookies in the ovens we had on board. They may not have been ideal for this use, but they could easily be used for this purpose. Once the cookies were done, we chose some children, gave them little baskets with the freshly baked cookies and asked them to walk through the aisles and pass out the goodies. The passengers were thrilled! Upon our arrival in Chicago it was such a joy to observe how the passengers said good-bye to us. They thanked us wholeheartedly and some of them said that they had just experienced one of their best flights ever. We could be sure that we had created a lasting memory and they would happily share their experience with friends and family.

The crew spent Christmas Eve in Chicago having dinner together at an Italian restaurant. The icy winter wind blew in our faces on the way back to the hotel and it felt as though it was shock freezing our faces, but the atmosphere in the city was special and unforgettable.

It's The Little Things

At the time, there was an advertising campaign running that had the title "Swissair – we care!". One of the posters showed a hand that was sewing on a button of a suit jacket. The message was clear: "We care – we sincerely give our best and if necessary, we will go the extra mile and sew a button on your suit."

It is important to notice that it is not always the VIP treatment, the golden faucets, the red carpets and the popping champagne corks that truly make the difference for the customers. On the contrary, it is often the small, surprising elements, the personal gestures that express human kindness, create a connection and therefore become something very special and unique. Again and again, I have experienced moments myself in which such an emotional bond was created between the customer and the service provider.

Just recently, I was on a flight to Dubai as a passenger when I heard someone singing "Happy Birthday" behind me. I turned around and what I saw was truly touching: Two rows behind me, there was a family with two little boys. Four crew members were singing to them. One of the flight attendants was holding a tray with two children's cocktails, his colleague was holding a birthday cake. But this was not your usual birthday cake: This cake was in the shape of an airplane. It was a moment I will never forget – and I am sure neither will the two boys. If you experience something this emotional in connection with a certain brand or service provider at such a young age, then this can have a very strong and sustainable effect. On other flights, pictures of children and crew members were taken on board to create a lasting memory – and sometimes they were even signed by the captain. I don't think that those pictures ever ended up in the trash can. On the contrary: They were probably carefully kept as precious keepsakes.

What Have You Done!?

As a customer, everyone experiences difficult encounters with service providers at some time or another: Misunderstandings, misjudgments and the individual behavior of the people who are providing the service lead to deviations between our expectations and what we actually experience. In aviation, there are many situations in which passengers do not receive the service they expected. Here are some typical examples:

// No window seat, even though one was booked
// Delays of all sorts
// Missing pre-ordered special meals
// Broken in-flight entertainment systems
// Families who are not seated together
// Too much or oversized carry-on luggage
// No meal choice available
// Cabin temperature is too low or too high
// Broken reading light or backrest
// Different aircraft type than expected

The way an employee in customer contact behaves in those kinds of situations is the determining factor and can make a huge difference regarding the overall customer experience.

Recently, I was flying back from Los Angeles to Zurich as a passenger. I boarded the plane, went to my seat in business class and prepared myself for the night flight. A while after we took off, I tried to activate the in-seat entertainment system, pushing the buttons that were built into the armrest. To my surprise, when I pushed one of those buttons, the cover of the control panel came off and

I could see the cables which ran underneath it. It was obvious that the cover had not been installed properly and I decided to get a crew member's attention. So, I took the opportunity when one of the flight attendants walked by, addressed her and showed her the loose cover of the control panel. She looked at me with big eyes and, in a voice loud enough to be heard by the passengers around us, exclaimed: "What have you done!?"

I told her that all I had done was push a button and that the cover had already been so loose that it immediately came off. She rolled her eyes, shook her head and said she would "write it down".

Based on my experience I knew that she meant the report book in which such defects and malfunctions are documented. That was our entire interaction. Neither did she ask whether the system itself was working, nor did she express any kind of sympathy for my experience. Instead, she made me feel like I had damaged the airplane. This was not exactly what I, as a customer, needed to remain loyal and committed. The rest of the flight was fine in every aspect. However, this small scene gave the whole experience such a negative touch that it even made it into this book.

CHALLENGES IN CUSTOMER CONTACT
///

For many companies, the markets have changed significantly over the last decades. Usually, customers nowadays have a head start on information when they come into contact with sales or service employees. In markets that become increasingly volatile and in which products and services become more and more interchangeable, there is one key factor that contributes greatly to a company's competitiveness: The human component. It is the employee working in direct customer contact who makes the ultimate difference – not necessarily by *what* he or she does, but by how it is done.

No matter whether your company operates in B2B or B2C (*business to business* or *business to consumer*): There is always H2H interaction, that is *human to human*. People always buy from other people because they trust them, because they are in contact with them, because they feel understood, accepted and taken seriously – with the exception of business that takes place exclusively online.

This makes the ability to establish real contact and build relationships a quality which is literally priceless in the field of sales and service. The salesperson transforms from being a provider of a service or a product to a trusted advisor by the customer's side, someone who helps him or her succeed. This also means that traditional sales methods and techniques nowadays usually fall short – any attempt of manipulation is quickly recognized by the customer. Due to the increasing demand for transparency, these methods have also become inappropriate from an ethical perspective.

In order to make yourself aware of the greatest challenges in customer contact, all you have to do is put yourself in the position of a customer – and we are actually customers ourselves all the time: At a restaurant, when we shop, when we hire a craftsman, or when we use the services of an airline. Also, based on the statement I made at the beginning of this book – "We are all service providers" – when I talk about customers, I always refer to both, internal as well as external customers.

The challenge for providers lies in eliminating bad customer experiences and in creating more outstanding experiences. In this day and age, a customer who is only satisfied with his experience is no longer automatically a loyal customer, as can be seen in many industries. Apart from customer behavior in the airline industry, this becomes very apparent in telecommunications: When it comes to mobile phones and the corresponding contracts, customer loyalty is declining. Even though customers are usually pleased with their service provider or device, they are still willing to switch to a new provider.

Another example can be found in the automotive industry. It is assumed that, depending on the brand, up to 50 percent of the highly satisfied customers are not loyal and thus behave like dissatisfied customers: They are willing to switch to a new brand. Conversely, that means it is no longer sufficient to merely have satisfied customers. If we want loyal customers, we need enthusiastic and emotionally engaged customers. This means, they need to be offered something they have not been offered before.

What does that mean? When you are engaged as a customer, you have an emotional bond with your provider. There are many good examples of that kind: Many Apple customers have an emotional bond with the brand, they even defend it against critics and they are willing to pay more money for their devices. What is important is how the customer feels during the interaction with a company or brand – whether it is a first contact with the call center, in a sales conversation, when making a complaint, or when requiring a service after purchasing a product. Emotions have great influence on our decision making. Most of our decisions are made unconsciously, based on emotions, and subsequently rationally explained. This means: Particularly in sales and customer service, the emotional state of your customer is a decisive factor. The behavior of your employees, on the other hand, greatly influences the emotional state your customer is in – or led into during their interaction.

Let me encourage you to ask yourself what kind of experiences your customers have when they encounter your brand at the various touchpoints. Do they experience enthusiasm, something extraordinary, unforgettable and phenomenal? Or do they experience average service and are merely "not dissatisfied"? When it comes to customer engagement and loyalty, there is a big difference between enthusiasm and non-dissatisfaction!

> What customers actually experience often creates the impression that the customers are not supposed to be won or retained. Instead, they feel as though the service provider would rather see them leave sooner than later. Terms that are often mentioned by customers in this context are rejection, ignorance, incompetence, arrogance, disrespect, empty promises, lectures, indifference, obtrusiveness, impersonal behavior, unmotivated behavior and so on. All these terms can be summarized because they all evolve around different levels of not being in sincere contact with the customer.

The underlying question behind this phenomenon is: Who is this about? Is this about me as a sales person or customer service employee or is this about you, the customer? Is this about what we have to offer, about how great we are, about all we have accomplished, is it about our references and awards or is this about your questions and needs, dear customer? Knowing the answers to these questions provides a completely different attitude which in turn directly affects your behavior.

Let me give you an example: A while ago, I invited several insurance sales representatives to provide me with an overview of the services they offered and my options. I sat down at the table with one of the sales representatives and after a short welcome, he started his presentation. He pulled out slides and graphics and explained to me, slide by slide, what his services are, how great they are and what they entail. He bombarded me intensely with information, only talking about himself, his company and his achievements – for about 15 to 20 minutes!

He had lost me after the first five minutes because I was clearly under the impression that this talk was not about me and my needs, but only about him, his company and his achievements. What I thought to myself for the rest of his presentation – it was a presentation and not the dialogue I had wished for - was: "When is he finally done? And when is he going to ask the first question that is about me? When will he finally come to meet me on my grounds?" It no longer mattered how good the product was. My trust in this person and in everything he represented had been damaged right from the start and was no longer high enough for me to get excited about the product and the actual service he was trying to sell.

BREAKTHROUGH IN CUSTOMER CONTACT
///

When basic human needs and emotions are so important because they impact the quality of a relationship and the decision making behavior, then it is obviously worth taking a closer look at them and considering them in customer contact. In customer service, two of the five SCOAP needs described in the chapter on "Self-Exploration" are of particular relevance: Self-esteem and control.

Self-esteem
The need to be valued and appreciated as well as to be treated fairly.
Customers experience a lack of self-esteem or even a sense of inferiority when they do not feel taken seriously, ignored, excluded, or even humiliated and when they gain the impression of not being welcome or at least accepted.

Control
The need for autonomy, control and influence.

When customers gain the impression of not being able to make a decision or influence the situation and that what is taking place is not really about them, they experience a lack of control up to feeling an actual loss of control. This is something that absolutely is to be avoided in customer contact.

Instead, consistently make an effort to create and foster feelings of appreciation and autonomy. If the need for appreciation is fulfilled, customers feel taken seriously, important, recognized, welcome and valued. Autonomy is only given when customers can choose, influence and control the situation and thus experience a sense of being able to act.

Moreover, our negative bias – the tendency to pay more attention to negative things – also applies to our perception when we are customers. This means we experience a lack of appreciation and control with much more intensity than when we receive appreciation and control. When working in customer contact, it is even more important to place great value on meeting those needs in order to compensate and balance out any negative emotions. For you to be able to succeed in doing so, your basic attitude as well as your high personal competence in dealing with your own emotions and needs are of tremendous importance.

Ideally, you not only recognize a customer's wish before it is expressed, but even anticipate and fulfill it before the customer becomes aware of it. This anticipatory customer orientation is one of the strongest success factors leading to an extraordinary and unforgettable customer experience. Hotel chains which are known for their particularly good customer relationship management will remember your needs. For example, if, during your first stay there, you asked for a softer pillow or orange jam for breakfast, you will find a softer pillow on your bed and some orange jam on your tray during future stays with the hotel chain, without having to ask for it. With this kind of service, your need for self-esteem is more than met.

A while ago, I led a training program for several days at a conference hotel. After I had ordered some tea while preparing for the training on the first day, the next day, I was asked if I would like to have a cup of tea again. I was positively surprised. For lunch, I had pre-ordered the vegetarian entree. When the appetizer was served, the service personnel pointed out to me that the soup contained bacon bits. I was positively surprised for the second time. It is those small things that, as customers, make us feel like we are noticed and that make a real difference.

On another occasion, I called my long-time Swiss telephone service provider to find out if I was using the best service package they had to offer for someone with my usage pattern. After a quick check, the call center agent pointed out that I would indeed be better off with a different kind of package. She offered to immediately switch my contract, and during our entire conversation she was friendly and courteous – which I considered normal and to be expected. The thing that surprised me, though, was what came the next day. I received a hand-addressed envelope in the mail. It contained a hand-written card in which the agent I had talked to personally thanked me for my loyalty. In the end, this gesture contributed to the fact that I am and will continue to be a loyal customer of this company. There is indeed an emotional bond and I am even willing to pay for it – and obviously for the quality of the product – even if it means I might be paying a little more than I would be with one of their competitors.

Again, the iceberg principle with the factual and the relationship level applies, the "what" and "how": The "what" does not necessarily determine matters of enthusiasm, customer engagement and emotional bond because it is usually interchangeable among most service providers operating in the same segment. But the "how" bears incredible potential: If the call center agent had sent me a typed card or an email – surely, I would have thought of it as a nice gesture. But just the fact that she wrote and addressed the card by hand gave the entire act such a personal note that it touched me on an emotional level.

And this is what it is all about: Touching the customer on an emotional level and bringing him or her to a positive emotional state and attitude. First and foremost, this is achieved by putting the customer at the center of your attention – not just in theory, that is, but in reality.

Managing Customer Complaints

The supreme discipline in customer contact is complaint management. When I, as a customer, have a complaint or an issue, I contact the service provider. I have the expectation that someone will listen to me, take me seriously and will make an effort to resolve the issue. Most companies even include this aspect in their advertising campaigns that this exactly will be the case, should there be an issue or a problem with their services.

Reality, though, often looks different. As a customer, I can quickly tell if I will have to fight to have my interests met. For instance, when I call a call center and first have to enter all kinds of digits on my phone so that the respective employee knows whether I speak German, English or French. This is usually followed by music that has more of an annoying than a calming effect. Just before I get ready to hang up, somebody finally answers the phone – a real person, an actual human being! I give a comprehensive description of my problem and receive the answer: "Oh, for this issue, you dialed the wrong number." Or "I am the wrong person to answer that." Again and again, this kind of experience is reason for anger, disappointment and shaking your head in disbelief. If customers reach a point where they are under the impression of having to fight for their right or for their needs to be met – particularly when they are filing a complaint – then you have already lost the customer.

In the position of the customer, what do I expect at that moment? Of course, it is possible that an employee is not in charge of my particular problem. Only: What I need at that moment is someone who will listen to me and take my problem seriously. "Ownership" is the key word here. Someone who will listen and help me. If I have dialed the wrong number, the employee can still say: "I'm afraid you ended up in the wrong place, but I will be happy to help you and put you through to my colleague", or: "I will write down your number and make sure someone will call you within the next fifteen minutes." This is my expectation and this would get me to say to myself: "This makes me feel valued and appreciated, I feel noticed, respected and, above all, taken seriously."

A large US-American credit card provider conducted a survey which showed that the level of customer satisfaction was very low. Measures such as customer retention programs, giveaways etc. had practically not helped at all. Only the following change of the work process at the call center increased customer satisfaction – dramatically and sustainably: Whenever a call was answered, the call center agent – after listening to the problem – said: "I will take care of your request and will call you back within the next ten minutes. Is that alright with you?" This was something the agents said even if they could have provided the solution immediately. Independent of how much time the provider actually needed to resolve the issue or obtain some kind of feedback, the customers were called back exactly after ten minutes. Then, the solution was either presented or they were told that the company required more time to solve the problem. The effect of this simple measure was that the customers felt taken seriously because they were sure that somebody was taking care of their issue or request.

Needless to say, when dealing with complaints you are often faced with situations that entail strong emotional reactions. In those cases, recalling the valley of tears can help: When does the customer usually call when there is a problem? At what stage of the curve is the customer when reaching for the phone? Chances are great that this happens during stage two, in the phase of anger and rage. Now, independent of your role and function, if you are at the other end of the line and are talking to a customer who is upset because he has something to complain about: How much sense does it make to try and give the customer a technical and rational explanation of why something is the way it is, why, at the moment, nothing can be done about it, and why it is possible that maybe the customer himself has made a mistake? This would do little to achieve the desired outcome because the customer will not be able to understand what you are saying while he is emotional and upset.

Instead, empathy is important: Listening one hundred percent, taking the customer and the complaint seriously and showing understanding. Meet the customer on the emotional level by saying: "I completely understand why you are angry." Help him describe the nature of the issue in order to make him feel understood and to help him reach a different stage. That is, the phase in which he realizes that he does not have to fight for his rights, but that doors are opened for him and he is met with understanding and a sincere effort to find a solution to his problem. Upon this realization, the customer is able to calm his emotions, release some pressure and thus be quicker to reach the point where he can think rationally again and have a reasonable conversation.

Recovery Is Everything

The "Circle Members" were Swissair's top 600 customers: Frequent flyers and usually first class passengers. We had invited one of those Circle Members during our Maître de Cabine training to learn from his experience and integrate what we learned into our work as Maître de Cabine. It was a Greek shipping company owner who had this valuable dialogue with us.

We talked to him about how he perceived mistakes and shortcomings. To our surprise, he said: "It is completely normal for things to go wrong and may not be the way I expected them to be from a customer's perspective. It really doesn't matter who is or isn't responsible for it: Wherever people are at work, mistakes happen. It would be an illusion to believe that things always go perfectly and there is never anything different from what is promised in the glossy brochures."

In fact, we all know quite well that we are often promised much more than what we subsequently actually experience. And, to some extent, we accept that: When we visit the well-known fast food chains we know that what we find on our tray is not what we see in the pictures on the screens above the counter, where the crispy salad and the fresh tomatoes are sticking out from the crunchy burger bun. But we still go there – or we don't, for that matter.

In other words: It is not about mistakes not being made. What matters is how they are handled. What I remember the most vividly from our exchange with the Circle Member is the statement he made in this regard: "Recovery is everything." The crucial factor is how a problem is handled! The correlation between a customer complaint that is handled well and customer loyalty has been proven on many occasions: If a problem or a mistake was resolved to the customer's satisfaction, the subsequent customer loyalty tends to be higher than it was before. What might sound like a paradox at first is in reality a logical consequence: Even though the customer did have a problem, he was heard, taken seriously and he saw that someone was taking care of his issue. Even if the problem cannot be resolved, as an intelligent being, he is able to accept that without turning it into a drama – as long as he saw that somebody did everything within his power to resolve the problem.

Conversely, this means: If customer loyalty is higher following a successfully handled complaint than it was before, then every mistake and every complaint serves as a red carpet, as an invitation to build and retain trust. It is an invitation to strengthen the relationship, thus sustainably increase customer loyalty and commitment. An unsatisfied customer shares his experiences with his environment much more often than a satisfied customer talks about his. Taking this into consideration and the fact that our goal is to have engaged, emotionally involved customers who like to recommend us to others, it is within our power to turn a dissatisfied customer into a contented, engaged and loyal customer – just by how we treat our customer when he files a complaint and how we handle the problem. Or just the opposite.

Basically, there are three simple things customers need when they file a complaint, that is, someone who

// truly listens
// really takes them seriously
// makes an effort to resolve the issue

When these three requirements are met and the customer experiences them as real and authentic, that alone can lead to the customer reaching a point where he says: "You know what? I can see that you did your best, so don't worry about it. Thank you for making such a great effort to help me." And with that, the issue is quickly taken care of. By going along with and not against it, you de-escalate the situation. This can obviously be more of a challenge when you are dealing with big and severe problems, but when dealing with smaller issues and daily dissatisfaction, I have experienced this myself on several occasions.

A far as self-competence is concerned, it is pivotal that the employee who is faced with the complaint does not experience it as something personal, thus falling into a defensive mode or even becoming irritated by or sharing the customer's anger. This would provide the ideal grounds for the situation to become more severe and even escalate.

Surprise And Goodwill
Two other factors for success in dealing with complaints are "surprise" and "goodwill". When you think back to when you experienced a completely successfully resolved complaint, then it is usually about things that were unexpectedly offered to you as a solution or compensation. Actions that are shaped by generosity. If the food at a restaurant does not meet your expectations, it is not surprising or particularly generous when you are offered a free cup of coffee after your meal. You almost expect that. This means, it is a false conclusion to expect a customer to enthusiastically go tell all of his friends and family about how well his complaint was handled. You might as well skip the free coffee.

You have to think of something else. I had an experience with a tablet computer that had suffered some water damage. I took it back to the store and said: "This thing is not working anymore, there probably was an incident involving water. Is there anything you can do?" Despite it being obvious that the mistake was on my part, the salesperson's reaction absolutely blew my mind. He came back with a brand new device and said: "The other device really is no longer working. Take this one." To me, this was totally unexpected, incredibly generous and, as you can see, I still talk about this experience today.

Another example has to do with when we were building our house. After my wife and I had moved in, we had problems with our telephone service provider: Apparently, the phones that had been installed were not compatible with the installed system. After I filed several complaints and was just a step away from switching providers, we were told to choose one of the available and compatible telephone systems. The provider would then cover all of the costs for the purchase and installation of the new device. That was a pleasant surprise as well as it was unexpected and we are still customers with that service provider.

It doesn't always have to be something this big, though. Often, it is the small things that get us to rave about our experience. In this context, it is of the utmost importance to transfer a maximum of decision-making power to the touchpoints at which the customer comes into contact with the company: The employees who work in direct customer contact. These employees need some leeway so that they can be generous and accommodating when it comes to resolving problems, thereby retaining customers.

///

STOPOVER - CUSTOMER CONTACT

Use your own words to summarize what you have learned for yourself in this last chapter and what kind of information you consider to be the most important or helpful for you.

_____

_____

_____

_____

_____

_____

_____

_____

_____

Think about the findings you would like to transfer to your professional or personal life. What kind of intentions have already begun to take root and where do you see opportunities to put them into practice?

_____

_____

_____

_____

_____

_____

_____

_____

///

DESTINATION PRIVATE LIFE

///

Image 19: Destination Private Life

ABOVE THE CLOUDS

///

One of the biggest disruptions in my own biography was the grounding of Swissair, when in October 2001, the entire fleet was not only proverbially, but actually on the ground because the company had run out of money. For the employees, this was an absolute shock, as if a carpet was being pulled from under our feet. People collapsed, cried, got existential anxiety, partly because many pension fund assets were out of reach in a single blow. It was a very stirring time and many people were personally affected. Two documentaries were filmed about that time and several books were written about it. Many people didn't know what to do next.

At that time, I decided to close the chapter on Swissair and open a new chapter in my life - out of a mixture of hope and conviction that this would be a good moment to do so. And so, the end was actually a new beginning. Looking back, Swissair's grounding was a stroke of luck for me personally, as absurd as it may sound. I might still be Maître de Cabine today - and I don't know if I would really be happy in that position. Over the years, this profession can become a real challenge due to its irregularity and the constant travelling, especially as far as personal and private life are concerned.

For many long-serving flight attendants, cultivating and maintaining relationships with friends and acquaintances is a great personal challenge. It is in the nature of this profession that you travel a lot, but at the same time you have more free time than your friends and acquaintances who have other jobs.

In aviation, not only the working time is precisely defined, but also the rest period due to different stress factors. So, after a rotation of several days - for example to Japan or the American west coast - I had three to four days off before I went on the next flight service.

The schedules were communicated on the 25th of every month, so I knew what my next month would look like. My roster usually consisted of a combination of short-haul and long-haul flights, perhaps with a few days of reserve service in between, a pattern in which you had to be able to step in for a colleague within an hour's notice. In addition, there were corresponding free days. If I remember correctly, we had at least nine days off per month.

What made the whole thing interesting was the irregularity of the work schedule - no week or month was like the next. There were not necessarily days off at the weekend and public holidays were also not automatically taken into account. What we had was a so-called wish system: We could use points, which were credited monthly, to enter certain wishes, for example a flight to a certain destination or days off. These requested wishes were not guaranteed, but allocated by the system on the basis of the number of points you had and on the basis of seniority, i. e. the years you had already been in the air service: The higher the seniority, the higher the probability that wishes were granted.

Since I had no rhythm and no regularity in my work schedule and was not at home at certain times on a regular basis, it was important for me to actively take care of my interpersonal relationships at home. That was quite universal: Someone who works with this kind of irregularity, as in flight operations, must not expect friends and acquaintances to keep asking: "When will you be home, when won't you be there?" Rather, it was important for me to take charge of this mission myself and to actively take care of the relationships. This was similar in the air service as in other professions with irregular working hours: The danger of loneliness was quite real. Personal responsibility in building and maintaining relationships is therefore not only an important aspect in general, but was particularly relevant in aviation.

The partial anonymity of the constantly re-arranged flight crews led, interestingly enough, to a certain openness because you didn't know if and when you were going to be together again. Especially on long night flights I had very deep, open and trusting conversations, despite the anonymity - or maybe because of it.

CHALLENGES IN PRIVATE LIFE
//

I keep noticing how the development of the leaders I work with is directly related to their private lives. For example, behavioral issues or issues relating to aspects of emotional intelligence are often also of relevance in their private life.

I therefore encourage my clients to share the results of their 360-degree assessments and stakeholder feedback with their partners and to ask them for their opinion. In many cases, life partners agree with the results, both in terms of strengths and, above all, in terms of areas of development. When managers work on developing their personal and interpersonal competence, such as showing more respect, listening better, regulating their emotions better, etc., they can work on it at home and use their private environment as a learning field just as well as their professional environment. I frequently hear reports of partners being happy about how their spouses listen to them again - as an additional benefit of the coaching process and how a real dialogue takes place between them.

My colleague Chris Hunsicker, a US-American coach who I met and started to appreciate in a global coaching project, observed in his work that there seems to be a connection between a lack of progress in the areas of emotional regulation and intelligence in managers and their personal situation. In particular, such managers are much more likely to experience separations or divorces in their private lives. For example, men can be loving and understanding partners at the beginning of their careers. Then they have children at some point and the pressure of the job also increases as they climb the career ladder. These two situations often coincide. If the various aspects of personal and interpersonal competence are not worked on carefully, and if the corporate culture is predominantly male-led and highly competition-oriented, there is a risk that the pressure and the dominant behavior patterns shaped by the corporate culture will be brought home and thus burden or even damage the climate at home. This is why the development of the corresponding competencies among managers is so crucial - not only for the professional career, but also for the situation in partnership and families.

Another major challenge is the demarcation or reconciliation between work and personal life. While our grandparents and great-grandparents still had the advantage that work and the private environment were automatically separated, because work was finished at 5 p.m. or 6 p.m. and normally no boss called on weekends, today we experience a completely different situation: The transitions between private and professional everyday life are no longer clear and with the support of technology we have the possibility to work independently of time and place - but also to be reachable. This presents us with completely different challenges today. It is a matter of dealing with these facts ourselves, making decisions and being responsible for our time instead of being controlled by our technological possibilities and therefore being slaves to our smartphones.

Personal responsibility is one thing. The other is the social responsibility that companies have in this context: Since 2014, Daimler employees have been able to use a tool that deletes all e-mails during their absence and refers them to their representative so that the matter can still be dealt with. The employees "should relax on holiday and not read any business e-mails", says the personnel manager. Since the end of 2011, Volkswagen employees can no longer receive professional e-mails on their Blackberries half an hour after finishing work. The server will be shut down during this time, company e-mails can no longer be received. Only half an hour before the start of the next service are they rebooted. However, this regulation only applies to employees who work under a collective works council agreement. In Sweden, some companies have reduced the maximum daily working time from 8 to 6 hours, interestingly enough while maintaining or even increasing productivity. This means that in this case as well, the balance was restored or at least an impulse was given in the direction of an improved balance.

I would like to see a differentiated approach to the topic. On the one hand by strengthening personal responsibility and self-competence among employees and managers and on the other hand by introducing flexible models where everyone can live up to his or her own demands and needs in order to provide optimum performance for the company. This varies from case to case, depending on the personal situation. It also depends on whether someone is completely absorbed in his work and doesn't mind doing something for his job on weekends. I am interested in flexibility in dealing with life concepts and life models, so that there is no need for rigid regulations to separate work and leisure time. There should be different solutions and possibilities for different needs. The condition for this, of course, is that the individual knows his or her needs, i. e. is in tune with his or her needs. In my view, there is a great need for action in this area.

In this sense, it is not about work-life balance - which would mean that life and work are not the same - but rather about work-life integration. Ideally, work and life are not separate and do not compete with each other, but are different aspects of the one life we live. It is important that managers recognize, appreciate and exemplify this accordingly.

When we look back into history, work and life were integrated for a long time and not separated. People woke up in the morning, took care of food and other things and went back to sleep in the evening. They lived and did the things they had to do. Only with increasing civilization has mankind set special times for things that are not directly related to survival. With the industrial revolution, the idea of separating work from the rest of life also emerged.

I believe that in the next step we must leave the aspect of time and space behind and go one step further, namely towards total networking and independence. Whether I work at home or in the office, in the evening or in the morning, it shouldn't make any difference, as long as my life circumstances, including work, are in good and well-balanced interaction. Today I live a meaningful, fulfilled and integrated life. I am very self-determined, I hold Skype meetings in our garden and I spend time with my family. Technology allows me to work largely independently of time and place and to combine career and family to such an extent that each area receives the attention it needs. This is what work-life integration is all about.

In companies, it also starts top-down again when the top management and the management teams have enough personal competence and are able to shape their lives in such a way that the different areas are balanced and interconnected. Only then can the culture in the company change accordingly and subsequently only then can employees at lower levels also allow themselves to orient their lives accordingly. The main thing is to measure results - not the time spent working on them. This responsible use of the room for maneuver means being able to say "no". After all, what signals do managers send to their employees when they themselves work until they collapse?

Imagine playing with your child and constantly checking your e-mails. Everything suffers: Both the quality of your work and the relationship with your child. And because work-life-integration offers the possibility to do tasks for the company even late in the evening, it must also be possible, in the sense of a balance, to take time off when it makes the most sense for you.

There are certainly companies that are already successfully practicing such an attitude: In recent years, Netflix has become a market leader in video streaming. Part of this success can be traced back to a very specific personnel policy, in which, among other things, something was thrown overboard that is very important to most employees around the world: The annual holiday entitlement. A 2010 Daily Telegraph article made a big splash when Netflix announced that its staff would take as many days off as they wanted, when they wanted. And: It works. As a result, a significant upswing in corporate culture, morale, creativity and productivity was experienced. The same was done at Windsor Regional Hospital in Canada, where an experiment with unlimited holidays could be described as an absolute success even after three years, and the British entrepreneur Richard Branson has adopted the model in Great Britain and the USA for his Virgin Group and so far has not noticed any negative effects - on the contrary, business is as good as ever.

BREAKTHROUGH IN PRIVATE LIFE
///

As you may have noticed while reading, of course the principles presented in this book are valid not only in professional settings, but also in private relationships. It is not possible for you to develop your personal and interpersonal competence without your private life and personal relationships being affected by it. In my coaching conversations, personal topics come up again and again, because these often cannot easily be separated from the professional topics.

Creating Space In Relationships
So, especially in long-term relationships, it can become a challenge to stay in real contact and not just interact with each other on a superficial level. Particularly too much proximity can lead to inner demarcation, retreat and the building of walls where bridges would be necessary. It therefore takes a good balance between closeness and distance. In the long run, too much closeness can damage the relationship – of course, too much distance can cause the same kind of damage.

Again, it is important to be grounded within yourself first. If you are in a relationship out of an attitude of neediness, then you will probably have difficulties to distance yourself and make time for yourself, because you will immediately lack the closeness, recognition or affection of the other. For this reason, a good way to a healthy relationship is to first establish a healthy relationship with yourself and to give yourself the necessary recognition, approval and affection. In this way we can approach each other with a completely different attitude - namely an attitude of emotional independence - and be together in a pendulum movement between closeness and distance."

Many people still go through life as needy people in search of a partner who can satisfy their needs and make them happy. Maybe they are looking for someone who is going to be their better half - as if one half of them were missing. And when the two half portions have finally found each other, they form a consumer community together and disappoint each other in the following years - because the demands on both parts are simply too high. The demands on one to make the other happy, satisfied and ultimately "whole".

Instead, what would it be like if two people were to come together, each of whom is already one hundred percent? Where everyone is complete and makes sure that he or she stays that way? Two people who do not allow their relationship to merge them into a single one being, but rather align their independent paths of life with each other and allow themselves to overlap to a certain extent so that a third, common path emerges? Then it is quite possible that two hundred percent can easily become three hundred percent or feel like even more.

And so, I am convinced that many relationships suffer due to too much closeness and too little independence. I am not talking about selfishness and ego-centeredness, but about self-respect, self-esteem and the friendly relationship towards yourself. For only when you can give yourself the appreciation and recognition that you want from someone else are you no longer dependent on someone who gives you what you lack, so you are not a needy person, but act out of an attitude of wholeness and can approach the other person with a spirit of giving freely.

One of the most important factors here therefore is to create space. Expressed in the words of the Persian poet Khalil Gibran: "Let there be space between you and let the winds of heaven dance between you (...). Sing and dance together and be joyful, but let each one of you be alone, just as the strings of a lute are alone and yet vibrate with the same music (...). And stand together, but not too close, for the pillars of the temple stand alone, and the oak and cypress do not grow in the shadow of the others."

Time Flies - And You Are The Pilot

We all know that the only constant in life is change. Nothing is for eternity. The building you are in will no longer be standing in a thousand years. On the meadow where you lie, there may be a building in a thousand years. The whole world is in constant motion. Think briefly about the changes you have undergone in the last twelve months alone - be it personally, in your private and family life, at work or with your customers. And think about what kind of changes you will have to expect in the next twelve months.

Constant change is a law of nature. And yet we tend not to be very benevolent towards change, especially when it seems unfamiliar. In the worst case, it may even come as a surprise - perhaps the next reorganization in the company, perhaps your superior, who you liked so much, maybe your relationships will change ...

Many people tend to hold on to the existing and the proven, believing that it is better than the uncertain, unclear, insecure. This is one of the main reasons why we have such trouble with change: Because it often brings along a lot of uncertainty and associated insecurity. "What will this reorganization mean for me? Will I be affected - and if so, how? What will my new boss be like?" All these open questions lead to insecurity and uncertainty - and dealing with them is one of the most difficult tasks of all. Often, we therefore prefer to be confronted with negative facts and know what is going on rather than being kept in the dark and not knowing what is going to happen.

"When the wind of change blows, some build high walls, others build windmills."
CHINESE PROVERB

It is crucial that you are aware of the fact that you always have a choice and do not have to be a victim of your circumstances. You are not helplessly at the mercy of the things that happen to you and have to make your happiness and well-being dependent on it, but you hold the steering wheel in your hands. Time flies, and you are the pilot. So, you can evaluate each change differently and deal with it accordingly. You have the power of choice: You can choose what you want to focus your attention on and what you want to concentrate on. You have the power to decide what meaning you give to things, situations or events. And you can choose how you want to react and deal with it. You can choose what you do or don't do. And only a small part of your personal satisfaction and happiness, whichever way you define it, is really related to what is happening to you. Most of it is determined by how you deal with it.

In his 2005 Stanford address to university graduates, Steve Jobs said: "You can't connect the dots looking forward; you can only connect them looking backward." You only recognize the connections in retrospect. The challenge, however, is that you have to live life forward, in the dense fog that denies you a view of the future. The past can be a valuable resource in dealing with change, namely looking back and thinking: "What have I already successfully mastered in my past? Where in my own biography have there been situations or experiences that I had perceived as very negative and stressful, but which in retrospect resulted in opportunities and possibilities for me?"

Not everything bad that happens to you, happens to harm you. With the insights I have gained from my own biography and the disruptions it contains, I would like to encourage you to look ahead with your own eyes, trusting that everything that happens to you will turn out to be important and correct at a certain point in time.

In a nutshell: It is not the things that happen to you that contribute to whether you are doing well or feeling bad, but how you think about it: Do you see the threats and dangers that lie in change above all, or do you recognize the opportunities and possibilities that lie in it?

Gratitude As An Attitude To Life

Are you just trying to survive? Or do you want to live life to the fullest, be content and be happy? Then you should also increasingly and consciously perceive the positive aspects of your life, pay more attention to them and enjoy them. And be grateful for them. For gratitude is a strong pillar of a happy and contented life.

Father David Steindl-Rast[48] writes: "The root of all happiness is gratitude. We tend to misunderstand this connection between happiness and gratitude. We notice that happy people are grateful and we assume that they are grateful for their happiness. And exactly the opposite is the case: Their happiness springs from their gratitude. "If you have all the happiness in the world and take it for granted, you won't experience happiness."[49]

I experience this again and again in conversations - be it in coaching, in management discussions or in exchange with my clients, seminar participants and customers: For many people, happiness and satisfaction are the result of external circumstances. This means that they are happy and content . . .

// ... *when* they get the job they've been wanting.
// ... *when* they finally get promoted.
// ... *when* they have finally found their dream partner.
// ... *when* their children have finally grown up.
// ... *when* they finally retire.
// ... *when* others finally accept them the way they are.
// ... when, when, when.

It is one of the greatest diseases of Western civilization to make happiness and contentment dependent on external - and in particular material - circumstances, in the belief of "more = better". Because what happens when these conditions actually occur, so that you would have to be able to say: "Am I now happy and content"? If you continue to make your satisfaction dependent on external circumstances, you will hardly ever be satisfied. Because once you have the new car, the new job, the new situation, the first honeymoon period is over and the happiness hormones return to a normal level, then it becomes reactivated again, the same voice that says: "I will be happy and satisfied if . . . ". And then there will be another condition that has to be met before you can be happy and content. It's endless. Because we make it about the form, not the content.

It is certainly legitimate to think that all this is important and all these factors can, of course, have an impact on the quality of life up to a certain point. But actually, in the end they are only of relative importance for our happiness. I have had long and profound conversations with more than enough people who have practically achieved everything at the material level of living conditions, who earn very high six or even seven-digit annual salaries and still suffer from existential fears. Despite their prosperity, they are unhappy, dissatisfied, depressed or even stressed. Although their circumstances actually offer everything that others cannot even imagine - success without being happy is ultimately not worth much.

This is not about jumping around with a constant grin on your face. Rather, it is about a state of contentment, a state of relaxed, serene presence in the here and now, independent of what is going around you. I understand happiness as a feeling of contentment and inner peace. Moments of bliss can then arise on the fertile ground of this contentment.

I worked for a circus for a year and a half in my early twenties and lived in a caravan during that time. Looking back, I was no more and no less satisfied during that time than I am today. And this is true for many people. So, say goodbye to the assumption that contentment and happiness are solely a result of external circumstances. Instead, open yourself to the thought that happiness and contentment is a decision. A decision you can make yourself. Any time and anew every day.

What kind of attitude do you want to have today, towards yourself, other people, life or work? Do you adopt a positive, contented, compassionate, generous and grateful attitude? Or do you see yourself as a victim of external circumstances and constantly complain about other people behaving badly towards you? And now think about what effect it will have on your environment if you are having a satisfied and happy attitude towards life: What will you radiate and what can you achieve with it? What kind of influence will you have on yourself - and on others?

Of course, this does not mean that you cannot lose this basic feeling of satisfaction every once in a while. The question is: Can you keep realigning yourself? Can you consistently orient yourself inwardly and adjust your inner balance again and again in a mindful, careful and friendly way so that you are feeling well and content?

Recommendations For Greater Dissatisfaction

With a twinkle, I would like to summarize a few recommendations you can adhere to in order to obtain greater dissatisfaction. Should you desire to definitely become and stay genuinely dissatisfied and unhappy, continuously follow these instructions:

Firstly: File a complaint

Complain about everything. Be as negative as you can possibly be. Whine and lament as much as you can. Whenever possible, make sure you pull other people along when you stare into the abyss by telling them how difficult, challenging and unfair life is.

Secondly: Criticize

Criticize others whenever you have an opportunity to do so – especially without being asked to. Surprise others with your criticism so that they are unable to defend themselves. Find something negative in everything someone else says or does. Search for and find the fly in every ointment. This way, you will be efficient in making yourself disliked and you will get people to avoid contact with you because you trigger massive negative emotions in them.

Thirdly: Compete with others

Show everyone that you are right and that you are better. Take every opportunity to demonstrate that you know everything better. Never leave someone else's statement or accomplishment unchallenged. Instead, give proof that you have always known better and done better. Walk through life with the conviction that you are the greatest and that you possess the wisdom and the power – and that everyone else, at the most, barely competes. Ideally, always start your replies with "No" or with "Yes, but...". This will make you really popular.

Fourthly: Judge

Evaluate, judge and comment on everything that happens to you. Label everything, every event, every statement you hear and every behavior you experience in others with a sticker that attributes a value to the whole thing. For example, you could repeat saying something like: "Ah, that is so stupid!", "This will never work!", "Who does he think he is? How can someone say something like this? What is he thinking?" Evaluate and judge as much as you can. All you have to do is follow your natural instinct for negativity and you will definitely feel bad and be unhappy.

Fifthly, the most important principle for consistent and guaranteed dissatisfaction: Compare

Compare yourself to others wherever and whenever you can. Look at the material things others possess. Look at what kind of car your neighbor has bought. Compare yourself to your supervisors and colleagues who make more money than you. Compare yourself to those who have already bought a house while you are still paying rent and living in an apartment. Compare yourself to those who fly abroad for vacations two or three times a year and not only stay at home for a few days once a year. Compare yourself to others, whenever possible, and you will see that it won't take long for you to feel significantly worse.

Making Others Happy

If instead, you would like to become happier and more content, then there is a plethora of studies available that clearly show: Whenever people act with generosity and altruism[50], by doing so, they activate regions in their brain that foster happiness. In a nutshell: Simple gestures of friendliness not only make others happier and more content, but also yourself. To me, working as a flight attendant was predestined for acting this way. There was nothing more satisfying than seeing how, after a long flight, people got off the plane, tired and moving slowly, but happy and thankful, even expressing their gratitude as they got off the plane. Likewise, in what I am doing today, there is nothing more rewarding for me than to see how others develop into a better version of themselves and thus make a more valuable contribution to their work or private life.

We are all service providers.

///

STOPOVER - PRIVATE LIFE

Use your own words to summarize what you have learned for yourself in this last chapter and what kind of information you consider to be the most important or helpful for you.

_____

_____

_____

_____

_____

_____

_____

_____

Think about the findings you would like to transfer to your professional or personal life. What kind of intentions have already begun to take root and where do you see opportunities to put them into practice?

_____

_____

_____

_____

_____

_____

_____

_____

///

SAFE LANDING

///

At some point, every journey reaches its end – so did my time at Swissair. It ended three months after the grounding. One of the most beautiful and moving experiences during that time was my last flight before I left the company. It was a long-haul flight aboard my favorite aircraft, the MD-11, that took us from Zurich to Dar es Salaam in Tanzania, where we had a layover of a few days before we flew back. I had a great cabin crew that included some members I had worked with on previous flights, and a great team in the cockpit.

Dar es Salaam was one of those destinations at which the crew usually stayed together and spent the time doing something as a group. Contrary to other destinations, where the time was spent differently after the arrival: In New York, for example, the crew arrived, checked in at the hotel, and then all the crew members quickly went their own way. Often, we only saw each other again at the time of "pick-up", when we all got on the bus that took us back to the airport.

The flight to Dar es Salaam went smoothly. We worked well together, the weather was fine, the flight was quiet. The highlight of our journey was flying over Mount Kilimanjaro, which is about 19,000 ft high and close to the Kenyan border. The pilots obtained permission from air traffic control to descend to a lower altitude and fly a scenic loop around the mountain. We were granted a lap of honor with a stunning view of the snow-covered volcanic crater. Visibility was clear and everyone was looking out the windows. It was a wonderful and unforgettable experience that, to me, felt like a small farewell present.

Over all the years, I had lost a piece of my heart in Africa. Particularly the countries of East and West Africa appealed to me. When I was there, I experienced everything with so much more intensity than anywhere else: The colors, the smells, the tastes, the music – and, of course, the people and their zest for life. Moreover, I had some of my most unique culinary experiences in Africa. Where else do you get the opportunity to try some freshly barbecued monitor lizard or python, or a grasscutter, which is called "Agouti" in West Africa? Yes, sometimes it is pretty good not to know what it is that you are eating – or to find out after the fact.

After we arrived at our hotel, we were able to relax for a while and enjoy the East African coast: White beaches, friendly people and great weather. Shortly thereafter we started preparing for our return flight: Packing our luggage, putting on the uniform and getting on the bus which took us back to the Julius Nyerere International Airport. I held the briefing for the crew at the airport terminal, close to our gate, as was customary at airports abroad where we did not have our own briefing rooms like we did in Zurich. After the briefing one flight attendant representing the entire crew addressed me: "Thomas, thank you for the briefing everything will be fine, we will make this a wonderful flight. For this flight, we invite you to take a seat in first class and enjoy the flight. You are our guest – let us pamper you!"

I was completely surprised and touched by this gesture and naturally very excited about flying home as a first class passenger. We walked to the plane, I helped with flight preparations and welcomed the passengers – not wanting to miss that last opportunity. Then I sat down in first class and enjoyed our flight home.

And, as if that had not been enough, the most beautiful part of the whole trip came shortly before we started our approach into Zurich. The captain made his usual announcement for the passengers: "This is your captain speaking, we will be starting our preparations for landing in a few minutes." And then he did something that I had not expected and that touched me deeply: He announced that this was my last flight as Maître de Cabine, that I had been a strong advocate for the company and had worked hard for it and that he would like to express his appreciation for all my hard work. In the name of Swissair, he thanked me and the entire crew and wholeheartedly wished me good luck, all the best for my future and continued success. The passengers applauded.

Tears were rolling down my cheeks and all I could do was keep looking out the window. At that moment, I realized that this was the end of a chapter in my life and I was letting go of something that I had grown to sincerely love over the years. I was deeply touched … and speechless.

After our arrival in Zurich I got up and stood by the door to personally say good-bye to all of our passengers. The people congratulated me and shook my hand, they thanked me for the nice flight and wished me all the best. When all the passengers had disembarked, I was asked to come back to the first class compartment. The two gentlemen from the cockpit and the first class cabin crew had opened a bottle of champagne, prepared some glasses and invited me to clink our glasses to celebrate the end of this era.

Take Off With Power – Make It A Scenic Flight – And Ensure A Safe Landing

Hopefully, all the impulses, ideas etc. you have found in this book will lead to a greater personal and interpersonal competence. I hope that, with these impulses,

I have been able to invite, encourage and inspire you to break through the sound barrier towards your next personal stage of development and approach some situations differently and more consciously instead of running on autopilot. Because at the beginning of any change process, there is consciousness.

This consciousness will further develop when you start applying what you have read. Maybe you have already started and you can already tell how your awareness is developing. Maybe you want to use the word "but" less in the future. You may realize how first, your awareness for how often you actually use the word "but" will increase. In the next step, you will realize in retrospect what you could have done differently in a conversation.

With increasing awareness, you will recognize during the course of a conversation what your options are and how you can direct and steer the conversation. Maybe you will realize how you could have expressed something differently after the fact and you will be able to correct yourself. With increasing competence, you will recognize your options prior to saying or doing something and you will be able to make a choice and consciously choose your action or communication.

It is all a matter of passing through a learning curve. Classically, it consists of four stages, plus a fifth one I personally like to add:

1. The *Stage of Unconscious Incompetence*. A pleasant condition: You do not yet realize that there is something you don't know.
2. The *Stage of Conscious Incompetence*. At this stage you know that there is something you are incapable of, which makes you consciously incompetent. Maybe you now decide to learn something new and reach stage three …
3. … the *Stage of Conscious Competence*. This is the stage you will probably reach first when applying the various principles described in this book - the stage in which you try to actively apply something. You consciously do something new.
4. With further progress, you reach stage four, the *Stage of Unconscious Competence*. At this stage of integration, you unconsciously apply the newly chosen behavior. You simply do things right and do so in a totally natural way.
5. The fifth stage of the learning curve is the *Stage of Conscious Unconscious Competence*. That means: You realize in retrospect that you unconsciously acted correctly. For example, you look back at a meeting and recognize that you unconsciously acted in a de-escalating manner. This allows you to reflect on the situation, pat yourself on the back and proudly take on the next challenge.

Change Is Pain – Leave Your Comfort Zone

Your comfort zone is the area in which you feel safe, the area you are familiar with and in which you are competent. It is important to have such a comfort zone. However, when we talk about personal growth, learning, development and making progress, this usually happens outside that comfort zone. Right on the edge, that is, a place that can also be called the "stretching zone" or "fitness zone". Just like building up physical fitness or muscles does not happen when you sit on the couch and put your feet up, but instead by applying effort and sometimes even experiencing pain. "Change is pain" consequently is considered one of the fundamental principles of change from the perspective of neuroscience: Change means pain in the form of physiological effort through the restructuring of neuronal pathways in the brain.

The stretching zone describes the area in which you experience something new and therefore learn. Due to the effort involved, this kind of new experience may feel uncomfortable, maybe even unpleasant. You may also feel insecure because the experience is unfamiliar. In the stretching zone, you can still control the situation and it can even be fun and exciting to act just outside your comfort zone. If this step is paired with excitement, you have the best environment for growth and learning. In short: The stretching zone describes the potential we have, but do not yet take advantage of - an exciting area!

Therefore, it is vital that, again and again, we consciously take a step out of our comfort zone and – ideally – become familiar with or even embrace the state of slight discomfort, knowing that we are in the process of gaining a new experience and learning. The encouraging part: The more often you enter the stretching zone, the more often you consciously expose yourself to the insecurity and uncertainty of new experiences, the more likely your comfort zone is to be expanded by that exact area. That means: What used to be your stretching zone a few years ago has since become your current comfort zone.

One example for this is giving presentations or speeches in front of other people. For many, this kind of situation is intimidating and definitely lies outside their comfort zone. Now, if they consciously choose to face their anxiety and repeatedly take the opportunity to present in front of others, they gain more and more confidence. Presenting then becomes a routine and thus part of the new comfort zone.

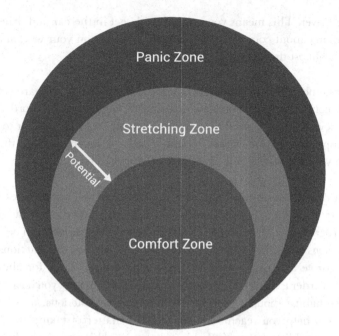

Image 20: Comfort Zone and Stretching Zone

When venturing out of your comfort zone, just make sure that you do not enter the "panic zone". That term describes experiences in an area for which you neither have the required skills, characteristics or competencies, nor the necessary potential. Such a step, too far beyond your comfort zone – like deciding to speak in front of 10,000 people in a stadium on a topic you are unfamiliar with – would take you on such thin ice that you would be likely to drown. If that happens, the consequence may be that the chances of you ever leaving your comfort zone again regarding that topic become very slim.

Successfully Building New Habits

Building new thought and behavioral patterns – in short: habits – is all about new neuronal paths being created in your brain. The objective is for the so called basal ganglia to assume control of these activities, that is the area in the brain responsible for routine activities and patterns which do not require much mental focus.

If an activity or a thought is repeated often enough, there comes a point where the basal ganglia take over and form a new neuronal path so that from then on, we no longer have to consciously think about what we do, but the reaction, behavior or thought takes place automatically. A good example for this process is driving a car. You probably do it automatically to a great extent, if you are an active driver. This means you can probably get in the car and drive from A to B, thinking about complex problems while you are on your way, and the car practically almost drives itself.

This takes time, repetition and, most importantly, patience. Prepare yourself for having to continuously execute new behavior for 60 to 70 days in order for your brain to develop the required neural paths and in order for a habit to be built. Many people give up after three or four attempts. To overcome that threshold, I call upon your patience – and, obviously, your discipline.

Research conducted on this topic over the course of the last decades has been able to prove that up to 95% of what we do every day either takes place based on habitual routine or as an automatic reaction to our environment. In other words: Our conscious willpower only influences about 5% of our daily actions. Hence, the inner drive and desire to achieve something only allows for about 5% of progress. In order to successfully continue on the chosen path, you have to develop supportive habits; thought patterns, belief systems, reactions, and behavioral patterns that help you reach your goal. It is a matter of taking the step from willpower to building automatic, habitual behavior. This is particularly important because the less energy and willpower you need, the less you have to think about something, the more energy and resources you will have to actually do it.

> ## "The secret of successful change is to focus all of your energy not on fighting the old, but on building the new."
> SOKRATES[51]

The principle of focusing mainly on what you want to do differently in the future applies: Focus on the new habits that are to be built and not on what you would like to get rid of. If, for example, you want to give up smoking, then do not focus on ridding your life of cigarettes. Instead, put the focus on what you will do differently in the future – or what you will be doing in those moments in which you used to smoke. Focus on building the new habit.

Creating – Preserving – Eliminating – Accepting

At the same time, you may want to preserve some things because they have proven to be helpful, you may have to get rid of some things because they have turned out to be obstacles – and, finally, there may be things you have to accept because they cannot be changed. These four options described by Marshall Goldsmith[52] in his book *Triggers*, are the backbone of the intentions you can formulate to successfully change your behavior:

Creating stands for the positive or conducive things you would like to create in the future. Creating is the prime example of behavioral change. When we picture ourselves behaving better in the future, we consider that to be an exciting process in which we re-invent ourselves. We create a "new me". This is appealing and attractive. The challenge is to actively take on the change instead of merely doing so as an observer. Do you create yourself or do you miss that opportunity and instead, are shaped by the influence of your environment?

Preserving stands for the positive, conducive things you would like to preserve or maintain in the future. Preserving may sound passive and trivial, yet it is a real choice we can make. It takes some soul-searching to identify what has served us well in the past and it takes discipline to hold on to it and not abandon it, only to replace it with something that is new, but not necessarily better.

Eliminating stands for the negative or obstructive things you want to get rid of in the future. Eliminating something is the most liberating and soothing action. Still, we often perform it with reluctance. Like when it comes to cleaning out the attic or the garage, we never know if we will regret getting rid of a part of us. We might feel we could use something in the future. However, maybe we are simply too attached to it – despite it being a hinderance for our development.

Accepting stands for the negative or obstructive things that you will still have to accept in the future. Most people tend to look at the first three options with more enthusiasm: Creating is innovative and exciting, preserving makes sense because it helps us not to lose sight of our good side, and eliminating appeals to our "either-or" nature which we use to drop behaviors which no longer serve us well. But accepting often is a bitter pill to swallow. Accepting is a strange player in the game of change. It sounds like a defeat, and to many, it equals enduring. When faced with a feeling of powerlessness, though, accepting can be a valuable step to take.

Sustainable Implementation With A Personal Development Journal

In order for the changes you want to make after reading this book to be implemented in a sustainable way, and for your experiential learning to take place in a systematic way, I recommend you start keeping a personal development journal. It is not a major thing and doesn't require much time or effort, while tremendously supporting you in the practical implementation and experiential learning process.

Make it a consistent practice to let the last task of your day be ten minutes where you sit down and think about the following questions: "What did I do particularly well today? What am I satisfied with, maybe even proud of?" Write down your answers. This could be something directly linked to a task you had planned on taking care of anyway, then put your focus on that. Or you can give yourself a general answer. Once you have written down this question and your answers, continue with the next question: "What did I not do as well today as I had planned?" Again, write down your answers. Then answer the third question: "What do I want to do differently in the future regarding this matter?" Write down your thoughts.

Lastly, I recommend you think about the following questions: "What am I especially grateful for today?" With the help of this question, you direct the focus of your attention away from the things you may be unhappy with to the things you are or want to be thankful for.

If you use your personal development journal as a tool on a regular basis, you will be efficient and quick in implementing the intentions you formulated. If you prefer, you can use it only once a week, or, initially use it on a daily basis and subsequently reduce the frequency to once a week. What matters is that you do it – with the frequency that works best for you.

Find A Sparring Partner

When it comes to successful change, self-reflection – that is, thinking about yourself – and formulating clear goals as well as intentions are critical elements and success factors - up to a certain point. You can do this up to the point at which you reach your own blind spots that were described in the chapter on "Self-Exploration ". Beyond that it can be very helpful to have a sparring partner who is able to support you in gaining greater awareness of yourself, reducing the number of blind spots, improving how well you use your strengths and growing in the areas that are important to you – which will ultimately lead to greater authenticity and sustainable happiness.

> ## "What we need the most is someone who will make us do what we are capable of."
> RALPH WALDO EMERSON[53]

While in the USA, this concept of having a personal coach and sparring partner has become a valuable and appreciated form of support over the course of the last 25 years, Europe is still slow to catch on to this development. In European countries, a problem and deficit oriented perception still tends to be prevalent in which something appears to be missing or in need of development. Slowly, though, there is a tendency for people to gain a resource and potential oriented perspective in which especially successful people have a sparring partner by their side. The sparring partner creates a neutral space for trustful, open and appreciative conversations where important insight can be gained and your own resources can be identified and tapped into. The comparison to top-class sports, which is where the idea of having a personal sparring partner or coach has its origin, is most fitting. Take a top athlete like Roger Federer who, despite – or because of – his success, works closely with a personal coach.

When you go back in time, discussing personal and professional issues with friends, family members or close confidants from the business environment is something that took place long before the term "coach" emerged. Obviously, these people can still be an excellent choice, given that you have that opportunity and access to them. Going back in time even further, kings often confided in their court jesters – the only people officially permitted to confront His Majesty with the truth. This goes to show, people have always been in search of a conversation partner who would not just listen, but also give them open and honest feedback.

The higher you go up the hierarchy, the lower the number of people in the company who will tell you the truth straight to your face and give you authentic, honest feedback. There is an actual probability that you won't be told the whole truth, that information will be held back or whitewashed. Not with bad intentions. This is particularly true for the emotional impact a superior has on his subordinated team. Your employees don't want to break bad news to you and find themselves ending like Hiob, who was killed for delivering a bad message. Or they simply don't consider it their job to provide you with feedback on something so personal. Or they would like to do it, but they just don't know how to approach the issue. For these reasons, many of my clients do not know for sure how their behavior impacts the organization they work for. They don't realize that they are not successful because of their behavior, but often also despite their behavior – and that they could easily be more effective.

Nowadays, having a personal coach is no longer a luxury. It can even be fundamental for being ready to meet and master the future challenges of your position. The stigma of the manager who appears to be incapable of handling things on his or her own is slowly disappearing, giving way to the image of a professional top-athlete who cannot only afford personal support, but also self-consciously chooses this form of support as a privilege, demonstrating and displaying authenticity and the ability for self-reflection.

By coincidence, I am writing these last lines while I am a passenger on a flight from Zurich via Dubai to Lusaka in Zambia where, together with a colleague, I will be holding a three-day leadership workshop for female leaders from various African countries. Contrary to my last flight with Swissair, the top of "Mount Kili" was hidden in the clouds when we flew by about half an hour ago. But I was able to see very well the two large areas of Serengeti National Park and the Ngorongoro Crater in Tanzania. So, the wheel has turned full circle and a wave of nostalgia rolls in as the plane goes into descent to Lusaka.

END NOTES

//

1. Charles Elwood Yeager is a former United States Air Force officer, flying ace, and record-setting test pilot. In 1947, he became the first pilot confirmed to have exceeded the speed of sound in level flight

2. Daniel Goleman is a US-American psychologist and business journalist who mainly became well known through his book *Emotional Intelligence*

3. A model developed by Harvard Business School Professor W. Earl Sa"er and his colleague James L. Heskett in the 1970s which shows the correlations between employee satisfaction and profitability.

4. Bernd Overwien, 2005

5. Maslow, A.H., 1943. "A Theory of Human Motivation A Theory of Human Motivation". P. Harriman, ed. *Psychological Review*, 50(4), pp.1–21.

6. SCOAP encompasses those human core needs which are neurobiologically based and deeply rooted in every human being. Neuroleadership, Habermacher, Ghadiri, Peters, Springer 2012

7. Antoine de St. Exupéry, French writer and pilot, Terre des Hommes, III: L'Avion, p. 60 (1939)

8. "A Wandering Mind Is an Unhappy Mind", Matthew A. Killingsworth and Daniel T. Gilbert, published in November 2010, Science 330, 932 (2010)

9. Linda Stone is a US-American author.

10. John Parr CQSW, CTA (P), PTSTA (P), MSc Thesis *The Feeling Wheel: A tool for systematic analysis of feelings*

11. MBSR stands for mindfulness-based stress reduction, an approach which consists of various mindfulness exercises allowing for an active stress reduction through more attentiveness and awareness.

12. Jon Kabat-Zinn (* June 5, 1944 in New York) is a retired professor from the *University of Massachusetts Medical School* in Worcester and received his Ph.D. in molecular biology from the MIT in Boston in 1971.

13. *Die 7 Faktoren der Achtsamkeit* by Jeannine Born, MBSR Trainer

14. Scott M. Peck, *The Road Less Travelled*, Touchstone, 2003

15. René Descartes (1596 - 1650) was a French philosopher, mathematician and natural scientist.

16. Viktor Frankl (1905 – 1997) was an Austrian neurologist and psychiatrist. He was the founder of logotherapy and existential analysis ("Third Viennese School of Psychotherapy").

17. Stephen R. Covey (1932 - 2012) was an American bestselling author

18. Gr. Philosopher, 50 – 138 n. Chr

19. Martin E. P. Seligman (1942) is a US-American psychologist
20. Actually: Samuel Langhorne Clemens, US-American narrator and satirist (1835-1910)
21. Elisabeth Kübler-Ross (1926 – 2004) was a Swiss-US-American psychiatrist. She addressed grief and grief processes and is one of the founders of modern thanatology.
22. Quote following Konrad Lorenz (1903–1989), Austrian behavioral scientist and Nobel Prize winner
23. Quote following Joachim Panthen, German aphorist and publiscist (1947-2007)
24. Albert Mehrabian (* 1939), US-American psychologist and professor emeritus at the University of California in Los Angeles. He became known for his research on nonverbal elements in interpersonal communication.
25. The word is "SILENT".
26. Achille-Claude Debussy (1862 – 1918) was a French composer
27. Interjections are words or exclamations which describe emotional reactions and are commonly used in spoken language.
28. Maya Angelou (1928 – 2014) was a US-American writer, professor and civil rights activist
29. John Mordechai Gottman is a US-American psychologist and professor emeritus of psychology at the University of Washington. He is best known for his work on relationship analysis through direct observation.
30. Amy Joy Casselberry Cuddy is a US-American social psychologist.
31. In her book The Friends of Voltaire, which was published in London in 1906, the author E. B. Hall puts these words into the mouth of Voltaire
32. On a Boeing 747-300, which was the largest plane used by Swissair at the time. On today's Airbus A380, there are up to 30 crew members on duty, depending on the airline and seat configuration.
33. Dr. Marshall Goldsmith is a US-American executive coach and author of various books on leadership and management
34. St. Gallen Executive Education Report (SEER) 2014
35. Dwight David "Ike" Eisenhower, US-American General and 34th President of the United States
36. Douglas Murray McGregor (1906 – 1964) was a professor for management in Massachusetts and is considered the founding father of contemporary management thinking.
37. Christine Porath, professor for management at Georgetown University
38. Gretchen Spreitzer, PhD, professor for business administration at the University of Michigan's Ross School of Business
39. US-American economist of Austrian origin, considered a pioneer of modern management.

40. Kazuo Inamori (*January 30, 1932) is a Japanese entrepreneur and founder of Kyocera and KDDI.

41. Sir Richard Charles Nicholas Branson (*July 18, 1950) is a British entrepreneur, adventurist and founder of the Virgin Group.

42. Paul Hersey, US-American behavioral scientist and entrepreneur.

43. Kenneth Hartley Blanchard, US-American author and management expert.

44. The silent-cockpit-rule states that, at altitudes below 10,000 feet, the work of the cockpit crew shall not be disturbed by conversations that have nothing to do with flight operations.

45. Simon O. Sinek (1973) is a US-American military advisor, author and motivation coach

46. Jacob Levy Moreno was an Austrian-American doctor, psychiatrist, sociologist and founder of the psychodrama, sociometry and group psychotherapy.

47. Kurt Tsadek Lewin (1890 – 1947) is considered one of the most influential pioneers of psychology.

48. Pater David Steindl-Rast was born in Austria and is a US-American Benedictine monk and member of the Austrian Think-Tank "Academia Superior – Society for Futurology".

49. Pater Steindl-Rast, David, *Gratefulness, the Heart of Prayer. An Approach to Life in Fullness.* N.J. Paulist Press, 1984

50. The adjective altruistic means "selfless", "unselfish", contrary to egoistic. Someone who acts altruistically is willing to sacrifice himself or his means in order to help others.

51. Gr. philosopher, ca. 470 – 399 v. Chr

52. Marshall Goldsmith, Mark Reiter, *Triggers: Sparking positive change and making it last,* 2015

53. Ralph Waldo Emerson (1803 – 1882) was a US-American essayist, author and poet.

ACKNOWLEDGMENTS

//

My sincere thanks go to all the people who directly and indirectly contributed to the creation of this book. These include in particular: My Family, Ben Schulz and the werdewelt team, Karin Lohner, Jutta Hörnlein at Wiley, Dr. Daniel Schmid, Jeannine Born, Daniel Suter, Nils Hämmerli, Sandra Kälin, Chris Hunsicker, Heinrich Scharp, Gordon Adler, René Senn, Paul Gutknecht, Werner Sohn, Stefan Geisser, Christina Bisschops-Kaltenbach, Gabriela Müller-Mendoza, all former colleagues at Swissair and of course to all the people I have worked with in my life. I have learned from all of you.

INDEX

//

A

Active listening 70, 77
Aikido principle 92
Approach 20
Attitude 76
Authenticity 77, 114
Autopilot mode 23
Avoidance 20
Awareness threshold 27

B

Beginner's mind 57
Beliefs 19
Blind spots 15
Bloom 116
Boarding 6
Briefing 6, 98

C

Circle of concern 42
Circle of influence 42
Comfort zone 170
Command & Care 119
Command & Control 116
Competitive advantage 3
Continuous partial attention 24
Create room 35
Credibility 77
Crossair 1

D

Debriefing 117
De-escalation 75
Development journal 173
Door selectors 6

E

Empathy 62, 77
Empowerment 110
Escape slide/raft 6
Executive center 50
Expect the unexpected 7
External perception 12
Eye of the storm 37

F

Factual level 79
Feedback 120
Feedforward 120
Fillers 72
Flourish 117, 118
Flow 38
Force field analysis 137
Forming 134

G

Galley 7
Gnothi Seauton 10
Go-Around ix
Goodwill 151
Gratitude 162
Grief cycle 47
Grounded 1

H

Halifax 125
Harvard Value Profit Chain 4
Here and now 39
Human doing 33
Human kindness 4

I

Iceberg   10
Ikigai   12
Inner critic   29
Inner weather   24
Interjection   72
InterPersonal Competence   5
Irritating expressions   67

L

Leading without power   108
Learning curve   169
Limbic system   111
Load curve   127
Low performer   118

M

M/C   1
Maître de Cabine   1
MBSR   26
Mindfulness   26, 27
Mindfulness-Based Stress
Reduction   26
Monkey mind   23

N

Negativity bias   25
Networking   84
Non-identification   32
Nonverbal   63
Norming   134

O

Observant position   27
One minute of silent review   7
Open loop   111
Ownership   107, 148

P

Panic zone   171
Paraverbal   63
Performing   134
Positive confrontation   86
Presence   26
Problem trance   92
Psychological safety   133

R

Rapid-eye-movement   59
Reactive patterns   89
Reciprocity   84
Recovery   150
Relationship level   54, 78
Relaxed control   112
Resonance principle   111
Respect   78, 82
Retreat   34
Reversibility   76
Role model   110

S

SCOAP   119
Self-organization   107
Servant leadership   4
Service factor   4
Service orientation   4
Silence   71
Silo thinking   128
Situational awareness   57
Situational leadership   118
Skill/Will matrix   118
Social awareness   55, 62
Social sensitivity   62
Sociogram   136
Soft skills   3
Solution Focus   78
Sparring partner   174
Standard operational procedures   99

STIR   90
Storming   134
Storyteller   23
Stress reaction   46
Stretching zone   170
Survival radar   25
Swiss International Airlines   1
Swissair   1
Symmetry   77
Synchronization   64

T

Team building blocks   132
Team development phases   134
Thought noise   23
Time of useful consciousness   50
Transitory Operations
        Information   6
Trust   115
Trustworthiness   84

U

Unruly passenger   2

V

Valley of tears   47
Values   17
Verbal   63
Views of human beings   108
Vulnerability   114

W

Work-life integration   158

BIBLIOGRAPHY

//

Covey, S.R.: *The Seven Habits of Highly Effective People: Powerful Lessons in Personal Change*, New York City 2013

Csikszentmihalyi, M.: Flow: *Das Geheimnis des Glücks*, Stuttgart 2007

de St. Exupéry, A.: *Terre des Hommes, III:* L'Avion 1939

Ghadiri, A.; Habermacher, A.; Peters, T.: *Neuroleadership - A Journey Through the Brain for Business Leaders*, Berlin 2012

Goldsmith, M.: *What Got You Here Won't Get You There: How Successful People Become Even More Successful*, New York City 2007

Goldsmith, M.; Reiter, M.: *Triggers: Sparking positive change and making it last*, London 2015

Goleman, D.: *Emotional Intelligence: Why It Can Matter More Than IQ*, New York City 1996

Goleman, D.: *The Hidden Driver of Excellence*, New York City 2013

Hall, E.B.: *The Friends of Voltaire*, 2013

Killingsworth, M.A.; Gilbert, D.T.: "A Wandering Mind Is an Unhappy Mind", in: *Science* Volume 330 No. 6006, S. 935, 2010

Maslow, A.H.: *A Theory of Human Motivation*, Radford 2013

McGregor, D.M.: *The Human Side of Enterprise*, New York City 2005

Albert Mehrabian, A.; Ferris, S.: "Inference of Attitudes from Nonverbal Communication in Two Channels", in: *Journal of Consulting and Clinical Psychology*. 31, Nr. 3/1967, S. 248–252.

Oberwien, B.: *Debatten, Begriffsbestimmungen und Forschungsansätze zum informellen Lernen und zum Erfahrungslernen*, Berlin 2001

Parr, J., *MSc Thesis: The Feeling Wheel: A tool for systematic analysis of feelings*

Peck, S.M.: *The Road Less Travelled - A New Psychology of Love, Traditional Values and Spiritual Growth*, London 2003

Porath, C; Spreitzer, G.: "The Value of Happiness", in: *Harvard Business Manager*, Januar-Februar 2012

Steindl-Rast, D., Pater: *Gratefulness, the Heart of Prayer*, New York 1984

THOMAS GELMI

//

Thomas Gelmi is an expert in personal and interpersonal competence and creates value for his clients as an executive coach, facilitator and sparring partner. He works for companies of all sizes, across industries and cultures – from Europe to the USA and Canada to the Gulf region, Southeast Asia and Australia. His clients include companies such as Siemens, Roche, Credit Suisse, Accenture and many more. He has been providing his services for many years, drawing on experience from three particular stages in his biography: seven years of international cabin crew management and training at Swissair, eight years as an operational manager of an internationally active consulting company with a focus on leadership development in sales, and nine years in various care institutions as a team leader and trained specialist for providing first care to individuals affected by major accidents and extreme events.

Printed in the United States
By Bookmasters